LEADERSHIP
UNLOCKED

WHAT THE TOP 1% IN NETWORK MARKETING DO DIFFERENTLY

LEADERSHIP
UNLOCKED

WHAT THE TOP 1% IN NETWORK MARKETING DO DIFFERENTLY

TGON Publishing

TGON Publishing

CONTENTS

INTRODUCTION

When Rob asked me to be part of this project, I didn't hesitate for a second. Why? Because I know the power of collaboration in this profession.

Between us, Rob and I have poured decades into building, leading, training, and supporting this incredible industry. But the real power of this book isn't in our names. It's in the voices you're about to hear.

Inside these pages, you'll find lessons from leaders who have actually lived it. Not theory. Not hype. Real stories from people who built through the struggle, adapted through the changes, and found ways to lead when it mattered most.

I've always believed that one person's story can change someone else's trajectory forever. That's what this book is a collection of stories, strategies, and perspectives that will give you a spark to go further in your own journey.

So, whether you're brand new or you've been around long enough to see the highs and lows, I want you to approach this book with one thought in mind: *What's the one idea, story, or lesson that I can act on right now?*

Because success doesn't come from reading. It comes from applying. And if you finish this book and do something different tomorrow, then we've done our job.

Let's get into it.

— Frazer Brookes

"Don't wait to be ready
to be ready."

STEFANO ORRU

Accolades

- Built a team of over 60,000 people in Europe

- Consistently generates 20,000+ new customers every month

- Runs a business where 90% of sales come from customers (10:1 customer-to-distributor ratio)

- Pioneer of online strategies since 2014, building exclusively through social media

- Helped hundreds of people become full-time professionals in network marketing

- Earned more than $5 million in commissions

YOUR BRAIN IS FULL.
THAT'S WHY YOU'RE BROKE.

The Overload Problem

You don't have an action problem. You have an overload problem.

"Drowning in information and starving for execution" — that's how one of my top team leaders described the state of her downline. She wasn't wrong. The most dangerous place for a network marketer isn't the marketplace. It's being stuck in their own overstuffed head.

I once coached a distributor who had everything — every course, every book, every podcast, every training recording since 2014 neatly saved in Google Drive. She could quote top leaders word-for-word. She knew the scripts, the compensation plan, the neuroscience behind rapport-building, and even the color psychology of Instagram posts. There was just one small issue: in the 18 months she'd been in business, she'd never signed a single customer.

When I asked her why, she said, "I'm just not ready yet. I want to make sure I know everything before I start."

That's when I told her:
"Your brain is already full. And it's exactly why your bank account is empty."

Coach's Notes – Rob & Frazer
This is such a strong story. Leaders will immediately see themselves or their teams in the distributor you described. You highlight the brutal truth: knowledge without action produces nothing.

Action Item

- Audit your "saved" content — delete at least 50% of trainings, notes, and resources you've been hoarding but never used.

- Write down the top 3 actions you can take right now without learning anything new.

The Whiteboard Attitude

In network marketing, the obsession with knowing everything before acting is one of the biggest business killers. The truth? You don't need more information. You need more action.

People think that success is about collecting every skill, every strategy, every tip all at once. But the more you stuff into your mind without using it, the more you dilute your ability to act with clarity and confidence.

I can't stand it when someone says, "Yeah, I know that." Those four words are the biggest wall between you and your results. In this business, the moment you think you already know it all, you shut the door on learning and on growth.

When you start a business like this, adopt The Whiteboard Attitude: wipe everything clean. Erase what you think you know, and let your mentor write new, proven strategies on your blank board. Because a cluttered whiteboard can't hold the map to your success.

Coach's Notes – Rob & Frazer
The "Whiteboard Attitude" is gold. Leaders often get stuck because they think they already know it all. This concept resets the posture: stay teachable, stay empty, and be willing to rewrite old habits.

Action Item

- Take a blank sheet of paper and write at the top: "What I think I know about building my business." List it all. Then cross out anything you haven't applied consistently in the past 30 days.

- Commit to letting your mentor's advice override your "old knowledge" for the next 90 days.

The Paradox of Preparation

Once, I had a girl in my business who didn't even speak Italian fluently. She had moved from another country, didn't know all the product details, the certifications, the science, or the studies behind them. What she did have was her personal experience — she had used the products, gotten results, and believed in what she was sharing.

So, she started talking. She shared her story, she had conversations, she connected with people. And guess what? She made a ton of customers, all without having 100% comprehension of the language.

While others were still studying every ingredient and memorizing every fact, she was already out there building relationships and closing sales.

When I started my business, I faced the same challenge. My mantra came from a sentence I heard at an event in Las Vegas:

"Don't wait to be ready to be ready."

It hit me like a lightning bolt. I realized that readiness is not a starting point. It's a side effect of taking action. That mantra became my compass. Every time I felt insecure, unprepared, or tempted to wait until I knew more, I remembered those words and moved anyway.

She didn't wait to feel ready. She got ready by doing.

Coach's Notes – Rob & Frazer
This section is a brilliant example of principle over perfection. The story of someone succeeding despite language barriers proves that readiness is earned through action. Your mantra is one every reader can adopt immediately.

Action Item

- Identify one skill or product detail you think you "need" before starting... and take action without it today.

- Repeat the mantra aloud 5 times: "Don't wait to be ready to be ready."

The Netflix Problem

Think about how you watch Netflix. You grab a snack, sit on the couch, open the app... and then it begins. You scroll. You preview one show. You check the cast. You watch the trailer. You go back. You scroll again. Next thing you know, 45 minutes have passed, and you're still holding the remote with nothing actually playing.

That's exactly what most network marketers do with their business.

They scroll through trainings. They hop from one mentor to another. They compare methods, scripts, and strategies like they're picking a movie for date night. And by the end of the day, nothing got done. No conversations started. No follow-ups sent. No presentations given.

Here's the truth: the Netflix Problem is really a decision problem. You think you're researching and choosing wisely, but all you're doing is delaying action. And in business, inaction compounds just like action does. Every day you waste in decision limbo, you lose momentum.

If you want results, you have to pick something and hit play. Stop browsing. Start doing.

Action Item

• Choose one method of prospecting or marketing and start it before the end of the day.

Student Mode Addiction

Here's the hard truth: many network marketers are addicted to what I call "student mode."

It feels like progress. You're learning, you're in trainings, you're taking notes, you're following multiple mentors. But your results tell a different story.

If you measured your business by conversations started, presentations given, or sales closed — instead of hours spent in training — your scoreboard might be embarrassingly empty.

Personal growth is essential, but if you're using it as an excuse to avoid uncomfortable action, then you've turned self-development into self-sabotage.

Worse, the more content you consume without applying it, the more decisions pile up in your mind. Decision fatigue sets in before you've even taken your first real action. You end up busy but not productive. Active but not effective. Moving... but in circles.

Action Item

• Limit yourself to one training session per week. Schedule it, and don't consume anything else until you've implemented that one lesson.

- Track conversations started, presentations given, and sales closed daily for 7 days. Compare it to the hours spent learning.

My ONE Protocol

Here's how to clear the mental clutter, cut through the noise, and force your brain to focus on what actually produces results. I call it My ONE Protocol — because success often comes from doing less, but doing it better.

1. **One Mentor**
   Pick one voice to follow for the next 90 days. Just one. When you try to follow too many mentors, you end up with a buffet plate of conflicting strategies. Focus brings clarity, and clarity creates action.

2. **One Method**
   Choose one way to generate leads and close sales. Commit to it. Mastery doesn't come from dabbling, it comes from digging deep.

3. **One Goal**
   Pick one metric that defines your win for the month. Every action should pass one filter: Does this get me closer to my ONE goal?

Coach's Notes – Rob & Frazer
This is outstanding. Your ONE Protocol is simple, clear, and instantly duplicatable. It gives leaders a way to silence the noise and drive focused, consistent action.

Keep It Super Simple

Imagine waking up and knowing exactly what to do today. No scrolling through trainings, no comparing strategies, no second-guessing. You've got your mentor, your method, and your goal.

Action creates results. Results create momentum. Momentum drives the business.

And here's what makes network marketing powerful: you can start with no experience, learn as you go, and still earn money while learning. Mistakes are tolerated here in ways other industries would never allow.

So right now, before you read another chapter, watch another video, or take another note, decide your One Mentor, One Method, and One Goal for the next 90 days.

Because the moment you stop overloading your brain, you start overloading your business with results.

"If you don't build your dreams,
someone else will hire you
to build theirs."

– Tony Gaskins

CASSIE ROWAN

Accolades

- Rebuilt a multiple six-figure income from the ground up in just 3.5 years with no formal training, just grit and determination

- Featured as a keynote speaker on stages across the U.K., U.S.A. & Europe, inspiring audiences to take action

- Successfully grown and led two of the largest organisations in different markets, as well as multiple others worldwide, creating unstoppable momentum

- Helped thousands of people achieve financial freedom by mentoring them into building sustainable passive incomes through leadership, duplication, and self-taught strategies

YOU'RE THE PROBLEM.

You Have To Close Yourself Before You Can Close Anyone Else.

The Truth About Sales

The truth is this: everything in life is sales. The sooner you accept it, the sooner you can master it. Most people don't want to hear this, but I'm not here to tell you what you want to hear. I'm here to tell you what will change your business, your bank account, and your life.

You are being sold to from the moment you open your eyes each morning until the moment you close them at night. From the coffee you order, to the car you drive, to the clothes on your back, everything you do is influenced. But here's the key factor: people don't want to feel like they're being sold to.

And that's exactly why you need to stop "selling" to them. Instead, you need to become so magnetic, so confident, and so sold on yourself that they lean in and ask for what you've got. But before we talk about how to get there, let's rewind, because at one point I didn't realise this myself.

Coach's Notes – Rob & Frazer
This introduction is bold and sets the tone perfectly. The reminder that everything in life is sales will resonate with leaders, but the real power is in showing that confidence and magnetism come from first being fully sold on yourself.

From The Stage To The Sales Floor

Long before I became one of the top income earners in my company, my passion was acting. That was my dream. I was lucky enough to tour with West End productions across the UK, living out what I thought was my purpose. But if you've ever been in that world, you'll know the harsh truth: actors spend more time out of work than they do in it.

I had no backup plan. I didn't want one. I was all in.

But passion doesn't pay the bills, and between acting jobs, I needed to earn. The only other things I was interested in? Fashion and makeup. Makeup! Bingo.

I told myself I'd take a temp job on a beauty counter. I'd look cute, paint faces, and leave whenever an audition came up. Simple, right? Wrong.

The moment I stepped onto the Chanel cosmetics counter in Selfridges London at 19 years old, I got a crash course in reality: this was serious sales. They had personal targets. Team targets. Average item sale targets. Everyone was out to upsell, close, and crush their commissions.

And do you know what? I became obsessed! Because that's where it hit me: everything in life is sales. And if I could learn to master it, I could control my future.

From there I went on to wait tables, I took roles in public relations, I was a shop assistant, PA... you name it, I did it! And in every single one of those roles, I was selling something for someone, whether that was a service or a product. I never got turned down from an interview after that temp job in Selfridges, because I quickly realised people buy people before they buy anything else. And if I was sold on myself and what I had to offer, despite my lack of experience and knowledge in nearly every new role I took, I could sell anything.

That's where the entrepreneur in me was born. I knew, if I could sell for other people the way I do, then why wouldn't I work for myself and keep all the profits?

So I started up my first businesses in my early 20s, and continued to do so, each time learning from the last.

The Lesson I Carried Into Network Marketing

Here's the irony: before I joined this profession, I was the biggest anti-network marketer you'd ever meet. Why? Because every time I was approached, it was sloppy, spammy, and unprofessional. I had copy-and-paste messages flooding my inbox from people I didn't even know. It felt transactional. It felt desperate. And I wanted no part of it.

But then something changed.

I decided to stop hating an entire industry because of how a few people were operating in it. I educated myself on what this industry allows for. I saw what was possible. And I realised I could help rewrite the narrative by doing the opposite of what had been done to me... That's when I understood I could use all my past experience in business, in life and channel it into network marketing.

Ultimately, you have to close yourself before you can close anyone else. If you're not 100% sold on what you're doing, nobody else will be either.

Coach's Notes – Rob & Frazer
This section is a breakthrough moment. Leaders will see themselves in your frustration with sloppy approaches, and your pivot to becoming an example of professionalism is a key lesson for the entire profession.

When Everything Fell Apart

Fast forward many years, during the global pandemic, I lost my clothing brand, what I thought was my "golden ticket." My beauty business was at a standstill. My dropshipping company wasn't dropping anything while we were all locked indoors.

I'd poured my life savings, my time, my energy, and my heart into it all, all while navigating motherhood for the first time with a 4-month-old baby.

I was exhausted. I was broke. And I was terrified.

So when my best friend came to me about this business (for God knows how many times in six months), I finally said yes.

But here's the difference: This time, I wasn't just "interested." I was all in. Or so I thought.

I came in as a "super recruiter," but I had no leadership skills, and I wasn't duplicating what I was doing. I thought I could do it alone until... I decided I wasn't doing it at all.

I stopped working on my business for a year and a half. I lost the team I had worked so hard to build. I watched people who started at the same time as me (or even after me) rank up, hit legacy incomes, retire themselves from corporate. There was no one to blame: I WAS THE PROBLEM!

So, instead of wallowing in self-pity, making excuses, or blaming others, I put my blinkers on and came sprinting back in to rebuild my business from scratch. I had seen what this industry had to offer. I knew where I wanted to go. I was sold on the business, on the vision, and most importantly, on myself. If they could do it, so could I!

And because of that, my excitement became magnetic. My belief was contagious. People felt it before I even opened my mouth. And I recruited like a beast off the back of it again, but more importantly I duplicated like one too.

That's the power of being closed on yourself first.

Why Most People Struggle In Sales

Have you ever walked away from a conversation and just known that the person you were talking to didn't even believe what they were saying?

Let me guess, you weren't sold on it either.

That's because people don't buy your product. They don't buy your opportunity. They buy your certainty.

When you are unapologetically confident in what you're offering, when you have absolute conviction in your own story, people feel it. And when they feel it, they follow it.

But here's the tough truth most people don't want to hear: If you're not closing people, it's not because they don't believe in what you're offering. It's because you don't.

Coach's Notes – Rob & Frazer
Your tough-love here is brilliant. Leaders often blame prospects, but you flip the mirror back where it belongs. Certainty is contagious, and you show that if someone isn't closing, they need to get sold on themselves first.

Four Questions To Close Yourself Before You Close Anyone Else

Before you pitch, before you post, before you speak, you need to get sold on YOU. Here are four questions I make my team ask themselves every single day:

1. Why did you start?

2. Why have you stayed?

3. Where do you see yourself going with this?

4. What have you found in the product/company?

When you take the time to answer these four questions with complete honesty and conviction, something shifts- not just in your thinking, but in your energy. Clarity replaces confusion. Confidence replaces doubt. And a deep sense of certainty becomes visible to the people you're speaking to.

I get my team to ask themselves these questions because they build a solid emotional foundation; when you know why you started, why you've stayed, where you're going, and what you've found, you stop trying to convince others... you simply become someone worth following.

The truth is, people don't respond to uncertainty. They follow conviction. And conviction only comes when you're fully sold on yourself. People feel your belief before they hear your words.

These questions aren't just for reflection. They help you reconnect with your purpose and lock in your vision so deeply that it naturally comes through in every conversation. Confidence doesn't come from knowing everything, it comes from knowing why you're here and where you're going.

Tonality And Sexy Language: The Secret Sauce

Now, let's talk about something most people overlook: how you say it matters more than what you say.

Think about the M&S chocolate cake adverts. The words are simple, but the delivery? Smooth. Slow. Deliciously confident. It doesn't just sell cake, it makes you want it.

Your tonality should do the same.

When you speak about your business, slow down. Drop your voice slightly. Smile when you talk. Let there be pauses.

This isn't about rushing through a script; it's about making every word feel like an invitation, not a transaction.

And your language? Make it clear, engaging, exciting.

Instead of:
"You should join my team; it's such a good business opportunity."

Try:
"Imagine creating a life where Mondays feel better than Fridays, where your work fits around your world, not the other way around. That's what I get to do, and I'd love to show you how."

See the difference? One sounds like a pitch. The other sounds like a possibility.

Sales isn't about pressure. It's about pulling people in with your confidence, your energy, and your belief.

The Process

Be human. Use voice notes, make phone calls, Zoom calls, or meet in person. Ask questions. You'll learn more from listening than from talking.

Pay attention not only to their concerns but to their questions and goals, and be sure to empathize.

Build trust and rapport. Share real examples, success stories, and testimonials.

Be clear on the benefits. Simplify. Successful people value their time; skeptical people value transparency. Be the problem solver: time freedom, passive income, additional income, career change. Solve it. Address objections quickly; education and confidence are key.

Support and reassurance. Let prospects know the relationship doesn't end at the sale. It's just the beginning of the journey.

Create a sense of urgency without sounding desperate. Explain the positive outcome of acting sooner: timing, paydays, events, training, their own schedule. Frame benefits as their advantage, creating a partnership rather than a hard sale.

Examples:

- What are you looking for from this business opportunity?

- What don't you like about your current situation, job, or income?

- Would additional income benefit your household?

- Does working in small pockets of free time suit your lifestyle?

- How long have you been thinking about making a change?

- If giving up some free time now means more free time later, would it be worth it?

- If you ask the right questions, you'll get the right answers, leading naturally into the close.

Everything Is Sales, But Start With You

Whether you're building a business, leading a team, or simply trying to convince your toddler to eat broccoli (probably my hardest negotiation to date), everything is sales.

But until you close yourself first, nothing else will work.

The day I got sold on me, my story, my vision, and my ability to lead, was the day everything changed.

And now it's your turn.

So remember: stop "selling" to people. Start becoming so magnetic they sell themselves to you. When you master that, you'll never have to convince anyone again.

These are the key fundamentals to any sale, but don't forget to have fun with it. Every "no" gets you one step closer to a "yes."

Excellence In Everything

Here's the truth nobody talks about: you don't have to be perfect to start, but you do have to take full responsibility for how you show up; especially when you're learning, fumbling, and figuring it all out. I wasn't great at every job or business I tried. In fact, in many of them, I was downright rubbish at first. But I showed up. I gave everything I had. That decision, to take ownership and commit to excellence even as a beginner, is what shaped the person I am today.

Every skill, every lesson, every failure became a building block. I didn't blame the game; I studied it. I didn't wait for a break; I created them. I took what I learned, refined it, and applied it relentlessly to build the business, the life, and the mindset I have now.

People will see the results and call it luck or timing. They'll see the outcome, not the responsibility it took to create it. But you can't have one without the other.

Excellence and persistence only show up when you do. You have to take ownership. You have to give your best. You have to stop outsourcing your potential and start acting like it's yours to claim... because it is.

So if you're not where you want to be right now, then yes, you're the problem. But here's the power in that: you're also the solution. And the moment you take full responsibility for your life is the moment everything begins to change.

"Freedom is not the absence of commitments, but the ability to choose – and commit myself to – what is best for me."

– Paulo Coelho

LEONOR FARIA

Accolades

- Multilingual entrepreneur, lifelong learner, and spirited traveler; started earning independently at 14

- Discovered network marketing at 17 and brings 30+ years of experience in direct sales

- Background in luxury hospitality, wellness, and beauty, with roles in 5-star hotels across multiple countries

- Proud mom to a 12-year-old daughter (her biggest inspiration and greatest adventure)

FREEDOM BY DESIGN: CHOOSING A LIFE THAT LIGHTS YOU UP

Intro:

Some people wake up, drink coffee, and slide into the day like it's on rails. Not me. I wake up asking: "If today were mine to design, what would I do?" That question (simple, audacious, terrifying) has shaped everything. Freedom didn't appear like a gift. I had to claim it, build it, and fight for it every step of the way.

There's a reason I didn't title this chapter "freedom by chance." Because I didn't stumble into this life. I chose it! Piece by piece, country by country, decision by decision.

I chose freedom when I walked away from a prestigious job in 5-star hospitality.

I chose alignment when I gave up the illusion of security to be present for my daughter.

I chose purpose when I started helping others create a life they didn't need a vacation from.

I didn't have it all figured out. What I had was a question burning inside me:

"What if I could live a life that felt like me and not just looked good on paper?"

And that question led me to network marketing. Not for an "opportunity," but for ownership: of my time, energy, and future.

Coach's Notes – Rob & Frazer
Your framing here is so powerful. You're showing freedom as a series of choices, not a random outcome. That is exactly what leaders and readers need the reminder that freedom is built through decisions, not luck.

At first, I had doubts. Coming from luxury hotels, network marketing felt foreign, unstructured, too informal, too risky. But then I realized something no job had ever given me: I could build something that didn't require me to leave my daughter behind, silence my intuition, or sacrifice my health. I could create income around my life, not the other way around.

The shift didn't happen overnight. There were fears, doubts, and a few "Am I completely crazy?" moments. A mortgage, a daughter, a reputation built over decades. All of it felt like stakes. But deep down, I knew something had shifted: I no longer wanted to live for weekends. I wanted to design my life.

Network marketing (the thing I once rolled my eyes at) came knocking with a suitcase full of surprises: freedom, community, growth, and fun. (Seriously... who knew making money could involve dance parties, WhatsApp voice notes, and team calls in pajamas?)

I realized this wasn't just a business model. It was a mirror reflecting who I was becoming:

- A mom who didn't have to choose between presence and purpose.

- A leader who traded scripts for soul.

- A woman who finally understood that freedom isn't earned, it's declared.

I started in network marketing at seventeen. Curious, energetic, and already dreaming of freedom. No roadmap, no system, no mentor, just flyers and ideas. I saw the potential, but I didn't know how to activate it. I had to learn the hard way: trial, error, and lots of "what now?" moments. But even then, one thing was clear: I loved people. Connection. Making people feel something... happiness.

Coach's Notes – Rob & Frazer
The contrast between your early days and today is a lesson in resilience. Many people quit when things feel unstructured or uncertain. You show that sticking with it long enough to align business with values creates lasting freedom.

My parents believed in experiences over luxuries. So whenever we had a window of time (and a tank of gas), we'd pack up the car and hit the road. No GPS, just my dad's mental map and my mom's steady hands behind the wheel. They shared the driving and the spirit of adventure equally. Weekends were road trips: Portugal, Spain, Andorra, France. Hidden beaches, mountain villages, winding roads... travel wasn't just fun, it was possibility. That spirit stayed with me.

Later I moved to the U.S., paused my career, studied, volunteered, and gave my daughter a front-row seat to life in action. Eventually, I could work... but daycare versus paycheck didn't add up. I didn't want to pay someone else to raise my child. I wanted presence. Flexibility. Meaning. Profit. That's when network marketing returned, not as a side hustle, but as a second chance.

Back then, I chased potential. Now, I am chasing peace. Not everyone understood. Personal growth was met with eye-rolls and sarcasm. But deep down, I knew why: I was becoming someone who could no longer shrink. So I stopped asking for permission. I got a divorce. I chose freedom. I chose my daughter. I chose me.

It wasn't easy (financially, emotionally, logistically) but it was real. And real, I've learned, is worth everything.

Newly single, self-employed, committed, I faced fear head-on. Every time I looked at my daughter, I remembered why I started. She watched me build from the ground up, learning she could do it too, without waiting for permission.

Freedom isn't sleeping in or sipping cocktails on a Tuesday (though sometimes it is). It's saying:

- "Yes" to a school field trip without asking for time off.

- "No" to a toxic environment.

- "Not now" to burnout.

- "Absolutely yes" to alignment, growth, and adventure.

Coach's Notes – Rob & Frazer
This breakdown of what freedom really looks like is a gift to the reader. You strip away the hype and show the everyday choices that actually build a free life. That kind of clarity is what makes your story duplicatable.

Network marketing done from the heart, isn't hype. It's honoring your values while helping others do the same. It's building something real, joyful, and deeply aligned. I built a business around connection, led with honesty and mentored from lived experience.

Today, I mentor people all over the world. Many of them women who once whispered "there has to be more" into their pillows. I tell them:

- You don't need permission.

- You don't need a perfect plan.

- You just need a decision and the courage to act.

Freedom doesn't show up wrapped in a ribbon. It shows up as a choice... sometimes scary, uncomfortable, even lonely. But that's not a sign to stop. That's a sign that you're breaking your pattern.

When I chose to start over (with a child to raise, a bank account that didn't always cooperate, and no clear roadmap), I didn't feel "ready." But I felt called. Following that call has taken me to places I never imagined, physically, spiritually, emotionally, financially.

I've built a business that supports my freedom lifestyle. I've traveled the world with my daughter, growing a business from beaches, airports, and cafes. I've laughed. I've cried. I've redefined what success means to me. And now, I invite you to do the same, whatever your version of freedom looks like.

Action Items: Design Your Freedom — Your Way

1. Redefine what freedom means to you.
   Not social media's version. Not your parents'. Yours. Write down what a truly free life would look like in your current season: emotionally, financially, spiritually. Be honest.

2. Audit your commitments.
   Paulo Coelho said it best: freedom isn't the absence of

commitment, it's the ability to choose them. Look at where your time, money, and energy are going. Are those things aligned with your dream life? If not, what needs to shift?

3. Take one bold, small step.
   Start that thing you've been avoiding. Message the person. Open the laptop.
   You don't need a perfect plan. You just need momentum.

4. Connect with people who make you feel possible.
   Find mentors, communities, and teams that celebrate growth. Not perfection.

5. Create from your story.
   Your journey (messy, beautiful, nonlinear) is your power. Share it. Lead from it. Build with it. You're not here to impress. You're here to inspire.

Here are some final thoughts that continue to guide how I live and lead every day. Consider this your permission slip to simplify, protect, and rise:

- Keep life simple. Focus on what truly matters, the rest is just noise.

- Don't chase people. The ones meant for you won't make you beg for their presence.

- Be around those who feel like sunlight. You don't have time for draining people or sneaky vibes.

- Take care of your body. Every lazy habit has a cost, and the bill always shows up.

- Talk less, feel more. Watch. Listen. You'll learn more in silence than in any room full of noise.

- Forgive quicker. Not because they deserve it, but because you deserve to be free.

- Own your life... with grace, guts, and zero apologies.

Freedom isn't waiting for someday. It's now. It's messy, imperfect, thrilling, and terrifying. It's the choice to speak your truth, chase your joy, and build a life that lights you up. Take it. Claim it. Design it. Because if not you, then who? And if not now, then when?

"The strongest force in the human personality is the need to stay consistent with how we define ourselves."

– Tony Robbins

REBECCA & MOGENS OLSEN

Accolades – Mogens

- 8 years in the network marketing profession

- Platinum-ranked leader and shareholder

- 30+ years of leadership experience in the medical industry

- Holds 5 black belts in karate and has taught for over 40 years

- Passionate about preventive health and helping others grow into their full potential

Accolades – Rebecca

- Trained social worker and professional actress

- 20+ years of experience empowering others through coaching, education, and performance

- Focused on helping mothers spend more time with their children while creating freedom through business

- Committed to inspiring people to make positive changes in every area of their lives

IDENTITY – HOW TO SEE YOURSELF AND OTHERS IN NETWORK MARKETING

If you want to know why some people succeed in Network Marketing and others don't, it almost always comes down to one thing: identity. Not motivation. Not compensation plans. Not even a skillset. If people don't see themselves as the kind of person who belongs in this business, they won't act like it—and they certainly won't attract others who do.

Identity is the lens through which we see the world—and ourselves. In Network Marketing, the shift from being "someone trying this out" to "a professional with purpose" is the single most powerful transformation you can make. Once people see themselves as someone who does this, everything changes: the confidence, the communication, the consistency.

You don't have to be perfect. You don't even need results right away. You need belief—and belief starts with who you think you are. It starts with your identity.

Mogens:
With a long background in engineering and the medical industry, I had no trouble understanding the products in our company. I could explain the science with ease. People trusted my knowledge—but still, many looked at me and said, "I could never do what you do." They did not see themselves as business people.

Rebecca:
As a trained actress and social worker, I was used to connecting with people emotionally. I could inspire and build rapport. But now, talking about nutrition and business? People didn't take me seriously. They saw the social worker, the actress—not the entrepreneur.

We both ran into the same wall from different sides: Identity.

If people cannot see themselves as successful in Network Marketing, they won't start—or they won't stick. And if people cannot see you as someone to follow, they won't take your lead, no matter how sincere or passionate you are.

Coach's Notes – Rob & Frazer
This is such an important truth. People don't quit because of the comp plan, they quit because of misalignment between who they think they are and what this profession asks of them. Identity drives belief, and belief drives duplication.

We all wear invisible name tags. Most people, when asked "Who are you?" answer with a job title, a family role, or a location. "I'm a teacher." "I'm a mom." "I'm from Denmark."

But what happens when you add something new to that identity— like "I'm a Network Marketing Professional"? Suddenly it feels uncomfortable. Foreign. Maybe even false. Because it is not yet integrated into who you believe yourself to be.

That misalignment between your current self-perception and your desired future role is what stops momentum dead in its tracks.

Solutions

Start with Authenticity

Don't fake it till you make it. Faith it till you become it. Begin with where you are—whether that's a new mom who wants to help others, or a science-driven engineer who's passionate about health. Present that real person with a clear mission.

Use the "I Help" Statement

Instead of saying, "I do Network Marketing," say:

- "I help moms who want more time freedom through science-based wellness solutions."

- "I help professionals create a second stream of income while staying aligned with their health values."

That's identity in motion.

Find Your Niche

Your niche is the doorway to your identity in the market. Ask yourself:

- Who do I understand deeply?

- What kind of problems am I passionate about solving?

- What's my unique perspective?

Understand Personality Styles

Referring to "Big Al" Schreiter's four color personalities can help your team see themselves clearly.

- Blue: Outgoing and fun, but can still be professional when identity is clear.

- Yellow: Caring and gentle, but can still lead boldly when identity is chosen.

- Green: Data-focused, but can still act decisively without every detail.

- Red: Goal-oriented, but can still slow down to show care when identity is intentional.

You don't have to change who you are—you just need to reframe it in a way that aligns with your goals.

Coach's Notes – Rob & Frazer
Brilliant practical tools here. Personality colors plus "I help" statements turn something abstract like identity into something simple your team can actually use.
Keep it practical and duplication follows.

Update Your Self-Talk

"I AM" are two of the most powerful words in any language. What you attach after them becomes your reality.

- "I am a learner."

- "I am a connector."

- "I am a professional."

Use affirmations not just to pump yourself up, but to anchor your identity.

Mogens:
When I first started, I followed the system and identified as a learner. I made early progress. But when my sponsor didn't know the next step, my identity cracked. Without growth, I doubted myself. Even when top leaders adopted us, I struggled to receive mentorship because I didn't see myself as worthy of success.

Then Rebecca and I had children. We shifted into a new identity: parents. For a while, we just showed up. We didn't quit, but we didn't rise either.

Eventually, we made the decision to own our identity as Network Marketing Professionals—not because of rank, but because of how we showed up daily. We invested in personal development. We even invested our earnings into shares of our company, which made us millionaires—not from sales, but from belief.

Your identity doesn't have to be defined by results. It is defined by decisions.

Coach's Notes – Rob & Frazer
This is the shift that matters most. Results fade, checks fluctuate, but decisions compound. When you decide to own the identity before the outcome, everything else follows.

More Solutions

Anchor Identity to Habits

You don't rise to the level of your goals; you fall to the level of your habits. And your habits flow from identity. Example: if I think "I'm not a runner," I won't run even with a 5k goal. But if I believe "I'm a martial artist," I'll show up at the dojo without question. Identity drives action. Habits simply express your identity.

Redefine SMART Goals

SMART goals can be helpful, but if they keep you in employee mode, they aren't serving you. Instead, define habits that reinforce your identity. When your identity is strong, SMART goals become automatic:

- "I connect with three people a day."

- "I learn something new about my niche each week."

- "I speak about my business with pride."

Teachability as Identity

When I lost my teachability, I lost momentum. When I reclaimed it, things shifted.

- "I am coachable."

- "I am open."

- "I am learning."

Teachability isn't just an attitude—it's an identity. An identity of willingness to learn combined with an identity of willingness to change.

Call to Action

So... who are you? Not your job title. Not your resume. Who are you becoming?

Network Marketing isn't about pretending. It's about becoming the person you were meant to be. Someone who inspires, uplifts, and leads. Someone who chooses their "I AM" with intention.

Advanced step for leaders: create an "Identity Circle" with your team. Have each person share one old identity they're releasing and one new identity they're stepping into. When identity shifts are witnessed and affirmed by others, they take root faster.

*"When your perception changes,
your entire life changes,
and miracles become possible."*

– Daniela Claudia Szasz

CLAUDIA LATTNER

Accolades

- 12 years of experience in the network marketing industry

- Built and led an international organization as a single mum

- Scaled first team to over 6,000 partners and 1,000,000+ in monthly volume points

- Made the bold decision to leave first company and a five-figure passive income to start from scratch

- Rebuilt career with a network marketing startup

- Within one year, new team became the top-performing team company-wide

BEYOND THE PLAN: WHEN SUCCESS MEANS WALKING AWAY

From Skeptic to Leader: My Unconventional Path in Network Marketing

I've had the privilege of learning so much from Daniela C. Szasz over the past few years. She has significantly shaped the way I work and contributed greatly to my success in network marketing and in my life in general.

You've probably heard plenty of amazing and successful network marketing stories, the kind that sound almost like fairy tales and leave you wondering, "That's incredible, but how?" You want that too, yet no matter how hard you try, you feel stuck. You go to the company events, follow your upline's advice, and try to implement everything you are told. But the results just do not show up.

If that sounds familiar, this chapter is for you, because my story did not begin with fast success either.

After finishing my studies, I got my first full-time job. My daughter was two or three years old, and I was deeply frustrated. I worked all day just to cover my expenses, and guilt constantly weighed on me.

I dreamed of being self-employed, of earning based on performance rather than hours, and of working from home. I shared this dream with others, but the response was always the same: laughter.
"As a single mom, that is just how life is," they said.
But I could not accept that.

At 26, I made a radical decision. I quit my job, gave up my apartment, and left Austria to travel through South America with my four-year-old daughter. I finally felt alive, spending time with her, discovering new places, and living adventurously. I promised myself: when I return home, I will not go back to a 9-to-5 job just to survive.

Strangely, during that trip, several people tried to recruit me into their network marketing businesses, in parks and on the street, but I did not understand it at the time. Then one day, my mom called, excited about an opportunity. She needed me to sign up so she could qualify for a free cruise. I did not understand what I was joining, but I wanted to help her, so I said yes.

And just like that, without a single presentation or explanation, I was in network marketing.

Two years later, I returned to Austria with one thing clear in my heart: I would never again waste my time on a job that did not feel meaningful.

But I did not know where to start.

Then my mom invited me to a presentation. I wanted to say no, but decided to go anyway. Honestly, I was the most sceptical person in the room. I asked everything.
How does it work?
Where do I find people?
What if I do not know anyone?

Something about it resonated with me: being self-employed, managing my own time, deciding how much I want to earn. I was curious, yet still skeptical. I did not know if I could sell a product or recruit even one team member.

Back then, no one would have expected me to succeed. I was introverted, anxious, and shy.

Still, I started. Not boldly. Not quickly. I found a part-time job for "security" and decided to homeschool my daughter. I started with network marketing, slowly.

And I quickly realized that I truly enjoyed it. Back then, I did everything the traditional way, no social media, and since I had spent the previous two years abroad, I had to rebuild my network from scratch. I started meeting new people, made new contacts, and began to find customers.

Within a few months, I had built a small side income of €300 to €700, and I wanted more. I wanted a team.

But I hit a wall. Deep down, I still believed this might be some kind of pyramid scheme, maybe not completely, but at least a little.

I spoke to people with enthusiasm, telling them about the opportunity. They were genuinely interested in the products and the philosophy, and they wanted to learn more about the business. Then they would ask:
"Is this a pyramid scheme?"
And I responded, yes.

You can imagine how successful that approach was.

I was not moving forward. Building customers was fine. Creating loyal customers was fine. Attracting business partners was hard. The real problem was my mindset.

So I began reading every network marketing book I could find, and again and again one word kept showing up: system. I needed a system.

I started asking. I asked my uplines, my sidelines, anyone I could. I kept getting the same answers:
"Trust the company."
"Go to the events."
"Stay excited. The company gives you everything you need."

I was already doing all of that. I was not lacking enthusiasm. I was going to every event. I was following every bit of advice from the company and my uplines, and still I was not moving forward.

That is when I knew something had to change. The answer was a system, but where could I find one?

So I started creating things on my own. I put in a lot of time and energy, but here is the truth: no matter how much time and energy you invest, doing a lot of the wrong things is still wrong in the end.

And yet, somehow, I made it. Without a system. Without a real plan. With willpower and enthusiasm, I managed to build a team of 200 people. There was no unification. For me, it was more frustrating than ever before. I had reached my goal, earning €1,000 on the side, but I could not teach my team how I did it.

These people trusted me. They wanted to make money too, but they were not moving forward. That is when I knew something had to change. "Trust the company" and "just stay excited" were not helping anyone earn money. I needed a system.

Coach's Notes – Rob & Frazer
Claudia just hit the core truth: leaders do not scale enthusiasm, they scale systems. Excitement can start a team. Only a usable, teachable system builds one.

So I changed the way I worked. My focus became helping my partners, the ones who trusted me, reach their goals. I created a system that offered real, structured training while helping people get their first customers and partners from the start. We combined that with our own team events so we could teach what mattered to us.

What once felt like "everyone doing their own thing" transformed into a unified way of working, a team pulling in the same direction. That is when the magic happened. That is when duplication began.

From a scattered team of 200 people doing about 20,000 in monthly volume, we grew into a team of 6,000 with over 1,000,000 in monthly revenue in three years.

That could be the happy ending. But it is not.

Plot twist: sometimes you have to let go of your success, be brave, and start again so that something greater can be born.

I loved my work. I truly did. Over time, I noticed the company was changing, and more and more I could not stand behind those changes.

It reached a point where customers placed orders with me and I did not respond for a week. That was not like me. I felt like I could not tell my partners and prospects the whole truth, and honesty had always been one of my core values. Much of what I was sharing felt like speculation. I was not satisfied with the direction the company was taking, yet I lacked certainty. I had growing discomfort.

That changed the day I found out the compensation plan had been altered, not in favor of the partners, and that the company had terminated several long-standing team leaders, including one of my uplines.

At that point, it was no longer speculation. I knew my company had a different side, and my motivation disappeared.

I had to make a decision.

Option 1: put on a smile, pretend everything is fine, and keep things running. Doing that would have meant betraying myself. I have always believed it is more important to look yourself in the mirror than to cling to false security.

Option 2: walk away from five figures in monthly passive income, from a thriving team, from the first company I ever built.

Coach's Notes – Rob & Frazer
This is real leadership. Titles and checks are easy to protect. Values are harder. Claudia chose values over comfort, which is why people will follow her again.

It was not easy, especially knowing none of my leaders would follow me and that my income would vanish overnight. The doubts came. Voices from the past echoed in my head.
"You did not build that."
"You just got lucky."
"You are benefiting from others."

I had no guarantee I could do it again. Deep down, I knew what I had accomplished. That experience and knowledge could not be taken away from me.

I had built that success. More importantly, I now had something I did not have at the beginning, a system.

So I jumped. Away from comfort. Into a new beginning.

The hardest part was not losing the money. It was saying goodbye to people, to leaders and friends, knowing most of those relationships would not survive.

Here is what I learned: you cannot hold on to what is already letting go. So I let go.

I started again from scratch, this time with experience.

After sending my resignation and making the announcement, I felt relief and excitement. Then an old fear crept in:
"Should I get a part-time job just in case?"

It was just a thought, and then it passed. The truth was I would not have had time for a part-time job anyway.

What followed was focused work: team building, customer building, system building.

This time, I committed to expanding the system, offline and online. I worked with new people and taught them everything from the ground up. We integrated a team app to make things smoother and more accessible.

Then something happened that had never happened in my previous ten years.

When you focus on what you are doing, stay out of scarcity, do what needs to be done, and trust life, there is no reason to be afraid. That is what I did.

I did not have passive income anymore. I had to build it again from scratch. This time, I was not tense or obsessed with immediate results. I found joy in the work. Somehow, that made everything happen much faster than the first time.

Before I left my first company, I had moments of doubt.
 Is network marketing really for me?
 Should I go back to a regular job?
 Should I try something completely different?

Those thoughts never lasted. I quickly realized I still love this work. I love educating people about health. I love supporting therapists in growing their practices. I love helping moms and employees build an income, small or big.

Just because a company no longer fits does not mean the path is wrong. Sometimes, you are simply no longer in the place where you are meant to be.

Coach's Notes – Rob & Frazer
Notice the pattern. Claudia did not fall in love with a company. She committed to a craft, a system, and a mission. That is why her results are repeatable.

Action Items

- Believe in yourself so the impossible becomes possible. If you spend your time admiring others but do not believe you are capable of achieving something great, life will not reward you with that greatness.

- You need a system if you want to move forward. Whether online or offline, without a system, duplication is nearly impossible.

- If you feel it is time to let go of something old, take that step. This does not mean jumping between companies. I was with my first company for ten years and only shifted when it was truly time to let go. Focus on one path if you want real, lasting results.

- Be coachable and open to learning. Have perseverance, patience, and discipline. Do not give up. It may take time to get where you want to be. If you quit, your chance disappears with it.

- Only learn from people who are where you want to go. Take a close look at what those so-called coaches have actually achieved themselves.

"Complexity is your enemy. Any fool can make something complicated. It is hard to keep things simple."
– Richard Branson

CINDY MCKNIGHT & LYNDSEY YOCOM

Accolades

- Built teams together of over 25k people

- Over 20 years of combined experience in the network marketing profession

- Generated over 80 million in sales revenues

- 7-figure earners

- Known for designing simple social media systems that scale

THE MILLION DOLLAR SECRET: SIMPLICITY DUPLICATES

Everyone's busy chasing shiny. The secret is staying simple enough that anyone can copy it, and smart enough that everyone wants to.

When we first started in this business, we thought we had to transform into someone else. You know the type: polished, professional, always with the right answers, the perfect presentation, the flawless social media profile. We'd sit on Zooms with people who could talk for twenty minutes straight about products or compensation plans and think, "That's what success looks like. That's what we have to do."

So we tried it. We studied, memorized, polished, perfected. We showed up as the "expert." And guess what? Very few people joined us. We poured out everything we knew, every detail, every script we rehearsed in the mirror. And the person across from us would politely nod, smile, and then disappear. No call back. No sign-up. Nothing.

We were frustrated and started to wonder if we were even cut out for this. Then one day, something clicked.

It happened with a friend. We were so exhausted from trying to sound perfect that we just didn't. We skipped the pitch. We skipped the polished version of ourselves. We just told her our story. The raw, real, messy, unpolished truth. We admitted we didn't have all the answers but were excited about what we were learning. Instead of explaining everything, we sent her a simple video.

And she joined.

That was the moment we realized it wasn't our "expert mode" that attracted people. It was our human mode.

Coach's Notes – Rob & Frazer
This is such an important moment. The fact that someone joined when you dropped the perfection act proves the real point: people connect to authenticity, not expertise. Leaders reading this will recognize how often they fall into the "expert trap."

That's when we discovered the secret: simplicity scales. Complexity kills.

And let's be very clear. The answer isn't who has the fanciest app, the slickest funnel, or the most cutting-edge tech. We have seen leaders burn themselves out trying to out-tech their competition. Tools matter, but they will never replace connection, consistency, and simplicity. If your business only works when it's powered by a NASA-level dashboard or a perfectly automated funnel, you have missed the point. Technology can support duplication, but it can't be the duplication. The second your process looks like it requires a marketing degree or a full IT department, people check out. It is not about out-teching. It is about out-relating.

And trust us, we have done the high-tech thing. We innovated tools, implemented them, and even buried them. They looked impressive. They even attracted people for a while. The raw truth? It didn't convert. We had to swallow our pride and admit that to ourselves, and to our people who trusted us. We painfully learned it is not the fanciest tools that win. It is the easiest ones. Because if a brand-new person can't figure it out in five minutes, duplication dies on day one.

Coach's Notes – Rob & Frazer
Your insight on tools is a wake-up call. Many leaders chase automation thinking it will solve everything. You make it clear: if the process can't be duplicated quickly by a new person, it's already broken. That's a lesson worth repeating across the profession.

We learned this the hard way. The more information we shared, the faster people tuned out. When we rattled off science or tried to sound like mini-doctors, they thought, "I could never know all that stuff." The smoother we got in conversations, the more people panicked, thinking, "I'll never be able to say it like that." And the more we showed up online as polished experts, the more people assumed that is what success required. Spoiler: it doesn't.

The lesson? Stop trying to impress people. Start making it believable.

The Walmart Run Test

One way we keep ourselves in check is what we call the Walmart Run Test. If someone bumped into us at Walmart in sweatpants, messy bun, no makeup, kids arguing in the cart, and asked, "How's that business you're doing?" could we explain it in under a minute without sounding like a robot? If the answer is no, we have made it too complicated.

That is why being the girl next door matters. Because the girl next door isn't intimidating. She isn't putting on a show. She is just real. And when people see her doing something, they believe they can too.

People Don't Follow Perfection. They Follow Possibility.

We once had a brand-new teammate who had no experience, no sales background, and was terrified to talk to people because she thought she had to sound like us. So we told her, "Don't explain a thing. Just tell your story and send them the video." She messaged five people that day. Two joined. Not because she was polished. Not because she was brilliant. But because she was believable.

That is the million-dollar secret. People aren't looking for experts to idolize. They are looking for someone who makes them believe they could do this too.

Coach's Notes – Rob & Frazer
This story brings it home beautifully. It proves
that duplication is about believability. A brand-
new teammate can win because she feels real, not
rehearsed. That is exactly what leaders need to model.

The Trap of Being the Expert

We will be honest, there is an ego boost in being the expert. It feels good to know the answers, to look smart, to get applause for being impressive. But here is the problem. When you build your business around being the expert, you build a business nobody else believes they can duplicate. We have seen it over and over. Teams that rally around one charismatic leader collapse the second that person steps away. Because people didn't learn to follow a system, they learned to follow a personality. That is not freedom. That is a trap.

Leadership Isn't About Knowing It All

We used to think leadership meant having every answer. Now we know leadership is about showing people where to find the answers. Your superpower isn't in what you know, it is in how simple you can make it for the next person. That is why we tell our team all the time: "Don't be the hero. Be the guide. Point to the system. Point to the tools." Because if you have to be the hero every time, your business will never scale.

Real Life is the Hook

Some of our best-performing social media posts weren't polished reels with perfect lighting and editing. They were filmed in the carpool line, sitting in the driveway, or mid-chaos at home. Why? Because they looked like real life. And real life is relatable.

That is the secret to showing up online without scaring people off: stay normal. Let them see the chaos. Let them see that you are still a mom, still a wife, still juggling life like everybody else. Because when people see your real life, they don't think, "Wow, she's perfect." They think, "If she can do this in the middle of all that, maybe I can too."

The Sweet Spot: Know Enough While Staying Normal

We are not saying you should stay ignorant. Of course you need to know enough to guide people. But here is the sweet spot. Know enough to lead, stay humble enough to be teachable, and stay normal enough to be relatable. Cross that line into expert mode, and you stop duplicating. And in this business, duplication is the only thing that pays.

What You Need to Know

Here is the million-dollar secret. It is not about looking the part, being the expert, having the perfect script, the flawless post, or the polished presentation. And it is definitely not about out-teching the competition.

The real test is simple. Can the brand-new mom who is juggling kids, work, and laundry look at what you just did and think, "Yeah, I can do that"? If the answer is yes, you have struck gold. If the answer is no, you have overcomplicated it. And when things feel too complicated, people eventually move on.

That is why the win isn't in perfection. It is in relatability. It is about being the girl next door. The one who makes people believe, "If she can do it, I can too."

That is the secret that scales. That is the secret that duplicates. And that is the secret that builds a legacy.

And trust us, we are not guessing here. We have done the high-tech thing. We built it, ran it, and even buried it. At the end of the day, it is not the fanciest tools that win. It is the simplest ones. The ones anyone can pick up, use, and repeat. The basics, done by real, relatable people, over and over again.

Action Items

- **Do the Walmart Run Test.** This week, explain your business in under a minute to three different people — a friend, a co-worker, and someone outside your circle. Pay attention: how many light up with curiosity versus tune out? If fewer than one in three light up, simplify it and try again.

- **Replace "expert mode" with "human mode."** Have at least one conversation this week where you skip the polished pitch and just share your story. Then note how the person responds compared to when you give the "perfect" version.

- **Point, don't perform.** The next time someone asks you a question, resist the urge to nail the perfect answer. Instead, point them to a simple tool. Track how much lighter the conversation feels, and how much more duplicatable it looks.

- **Audit your tools.** Take your top three tools and hand them to a brand-new teammate. If they can't figure them out in under 10 minutes, they are too complicated. Simplify or swap them.

- **Post real life.** This week, share one unpolished, real-life post — carpool lane, messy kitchen, or a thought mid-chaos. Compare the engagement against one of your more polished posts. Watch how people respond when they see the "girl next door" version of you.

I became an entrepreneur when
I realized it shouldn't take
an hour to earn $20.

– Unknown

JANE FREUND

Accolades

- Six-figure earner and mentor in the travel industry who grew her team to 1,000+ by doing it differently.

- Creator of a passion project in automation, helping network marketing entrepreneurs scale with systems and strategy so they can buy back their time.

- Co-host of the *Broke Is Boring* podcast, inspiring listeners to design lives they don't need a vacation from.

- Known for helping busy moms and travel enthusiasts build sustainable businesses without sacrificing family time, proving that success and a life you love can go hand in hand.

BEAST MODE WITH BALANCE

Most leaders in this industry will tell you to "sacrifice everything" for your business. I'm here to tell you they're wrong.

Before I found network marketing, I was teaching 5th grade. I cared about my students, but the workload was crushing. The papers stacked up faster than I could grade them. Meetings ate my planning time, and parent emails bled into my evenings.

I wasn't just tired. I was depleted—mentally, physically, and emotionally. And I knew if I didn't make a change, this would be my life for the next 30 years.

If you're nodding along right now, you might be where I was, working hard but not really living.

When I found network marketing in 2018, it felt like a lifeline. I saw people working from home, setting their own schedules, and building incomes that gave them choices. I wanted that so badly. I jumped in with both feet, ready to do whatever it took.

At first, I did exactly what I was told. I followed the scripts, joined the calls, and hustled the way the leaders told me to. I hit ranks, earned recognition, and checked all the boxes of "success."

But here's the truth no one likes to talk about: I had traded one kind of burnout for another. I had left the classroom cage only to build myself a new one.

A business that requires you 24/7 owns you. You don't own it. I had a mentor cancel a vacation once because she had so much on her plate. Hearing this didn't sit right with me. Isn't the whole point of this business so you can take a vacation without asking a boss for time off?

I remember telling my husband I didn't want to hit my current rank because I saw how much those leaders sacrificed, and I didn't perceive the income would be worth it. The ultimate freedom in this industry is to make money while you sleep, right? If you're trading time for money for the rest of your life while boasting about time freedom, I'd argue that you've been duped.

I was working late nights, answering messages at all hours, and constantly feeling behind. I told myself it was just part of the grind and once I reached a certain rank or income level, it would get easier. But deep down, I knew I was repeating the same pattern that had burned me out in teaching. Only now, I was the one making the rules... and I was still running myself into the ground. If your business only works when you're exhausted, it's not freedom, it's a trap.

Then 2020 happened, and my life flipped upside down.

I lost my dad to terminal cancer in just a few weeks. One day we were making plans for the future, and the next I was grieving the fact that those plans would never happen. As I learned to navigate a world without him, it all clicked. It was like someone turned the lights on in a room I didn't even realize I was sitting in.

Simultaneously, I became a mom for the first time in the middle of a global pandemic. It was a season of change, grief, and new beginnings all rolled into one. And it made me painfully aware of one thing: I was not going to miss my life for my business.

Maybe you've been told that if you just hustle harder, your breakthrough will come. I'm here to tell you there's a better way.

That realization didn't make me want to quit. It made me want to build differently. I wanted my business to give me more time with my family, not take me away from them. I wanted it to be the vehicle for freedom, not another cage.

I decided to take all that grief, all that perspective, and use it as fuel. Not to work harder for the sake of working harder, but to create residual income as quickly as possible so I could have choices, space, and time now—not ten years from now.

That's when I started building with what I now call Beast Mode with Balance.

I didn't invent the idea of working hard, but I rejected the idea that you have to work hard at the expense of everything else. Beast Mode with Balance means going all in during focused seasons, but protecting your health, relationships, and priorities while you do it.

Coach's Notes – Rob & Frazer
Jane nails it here. Too many people think success only comes from nonstop hustle. What she's showing is the next level of leadership: knowing how to push without destroying yourself. The greatest leaders create duplication not by burning brighter but by burning longer.

It's not about never working late or never making sacrifices. It's about making the right sacrifices. I'm willing to give up mindless scrolling, TV marathons, or errands that can be outsourced. I'm not willing to give up family dinners, bedtime stories, or the moments that actually matter.

You can't build a life you love by sacrificing the very things that make life worth living. My dad's passing made that crystal clear. There are no do-overs for the time you didn't spend wisely.

And here's the thing, when you do it this way, you can go harder when it counts.

When I lead a push period, I'm not looking for people who just want to stay busy. I'm looking for my runners; the ones who are ready to match my pace and lock arms until we cross the finish line.

One of my most impactful pushes started with a clear goal, a short timeline, and a rally cry. I told my team, "This is the season we go all in, together." We committed to daily income-producing activities, non-negotiable check-ins, and tracking our progress. We removed excuses before they could show up. Every leader knew exactly what to focus on, and every new person knew how to win from day one.

But here's the part most people miss: while we were in beast mode, I doubled down on balance. I checked in with my family before I checked my messages. I blocked off time for movement, quiet mornings, and real meals. I told my team to do the same because burnout doesn't build leaders, it breaks them.

Coach's Notes – Rob & Frazer
This is where leaders separate from managers. Jane built balance right into the push. That's what created trust, buy-in, and long-term duplication. Too many pushes collapse because people only focus on output, not sustainability. Her approach proves you can grow fast without breaking people.

That push brought me my core group of leaders. We celebrated the small wins as much as the big ones. We encouraged each other when it felt hard. We held each other accountable without guilt or shame. And because we built with balance, no one burned out before we reached the goal. In fact, my highest pay periods happen when I'm the most balanced.

If your family feels like they're getting your leftovers, this is your wake-up call to make a change before they start resenting your business.

How many nights are you trying to enjoy dinner with your family, but you feel your phone buzzing in your pocket? No matter if I'm focused on my business or family at that given moment, I'm all in. The phone stays upstairs from dinner through bedtime. Identify your non-negotiables and guard them.

That push didn't just move the needle, it changed the trajectory of my business. In two years of building this way, I went from 44 people in my downline to over 1,000 and was recognized as a 6-figure earner in my company.

It also gave me something more valuable than rank or income. It gave me proof that I could step away without it all falling apart.

This year my family and I went on a 120-Day World Cruise. Four months of traveling the globe, waking up in a new country every few days, and making memories that will stay with us forever. And you know what I didn't do? I didn't spend the whole trip glued to my phone. I didn't stress about whether my team could handle things without me. My business kept running because I had the systems, leaders, and boundaries in place before I left.

It was the kind of freedom I used to dream about, and it was only possible because of Beast Mode with Balance.

Now, here's where the balance part becomes real. It's not just about scheduling time with your family; it's about making that time count. If you're in a season of pushing toward a big goal, your family will feel it. And if you want their support, you have to make sure they still feel seen and valued.

One of the simplest ways to do this is by learning your spouse's and children's love languages. Maybe your spouse needs words of affirmation to feel appreciated. Maybe they need acts of service, like you taking something off their plate. Maybe your child's love language is quality time, and they just need you to play a game with them without distractions. Or maybe it's physical touch, and they need more hugs and snuggles.

You don't have to wait until burnout to change the way you build. When you are giving your all to your business, make sure you're also filling their cups in a way that's meaningful to them. That's how you build with balance instead of resentment.

For me, part of balance also means taking care of my own mind and body. When I'm in beast mode, I double down on self-care. I fuel my body with good food. I move daily. I drink more water. I get more sleep, not less. I set a firm business cutoff time, no exceptions. At first, it was hard. But by day three, I realized I was more productive during the day because I knew I couldn't spill work into my evenings.

I also train for time freedom before I take it. Before my world cruise, I intentionally stepped back ahead of time and let my team operate without me. That test run showed me where I needed to tighten systems or give more leadership to others. By the time we boarded the ship, I knew my business could not only survive without me, it could thrive. It was so successful, we decided to book another World Cruise because what started as a bucket list trip with my family turned into an incredible lifestyle.

Coach's Notes – Rob & Frazer
This is gold. Too many leaders only test their business when they're already gone. Jane tested her systems in advance, and that's why her team rose up. Duplication isn't just about scripts and calls, it's about building something that works without you there. That's true freedom.

If you want more time, more freedom, and more results, it starts with getting clear on what matters most and protecting it fiercely.

That's what I want for everyone reading this. To build something that doesn't need you 24/7. To work hard without burning out. To know you can take a vacation, a sabbatical, or even a day completely offline without your business crumbling. That's why you started this business in the first place, right?

Beast Mode with Balance isn't about slowing down your goals. It's about making them sustainable.

I share this message everywhere I can, including my co-hosted podcast, *Broke Is Boring.* It's where we talk about designing a life you actually want to live, breaking free from cultural norms, and building income streams that give you freedom instead of stress. Because I believe this industry needs more leaders who are willing to say, "You can have both. You can have success and a life you love."

If it costs you your health or your family, it's too expensive, no matter how big the paycheck. I've seen the rank advancements, the bonus checks, and the applause... but I've also seen the marriages crumble and the resentment. That's not the trade I'm willing to make. Beast mode doesn't mean burnout. It means focus. Sacrifice the things that don't matter so you can protect the ones that do.

Decide right now that you will no longer choose between your business and your life. Build in a way that gives you both. Protect the people and priorities that matter most while you chase your biggest goals.

The old way told me to sacrifice everything and hope my family would thank me later. My way makes sure they're thanking me now.

Action Items: Build Your Beast Mode with Balance Plan

- **Get Clear on Your Non-Negotiables**
  Write down the moments, relationships, and priorities you refuse to sacrifice. These will anchor your boundaries during push periods.

- **Plan Your Push Period**
  Choose a clear goal, set a short timeline, and outline the exact daily actions that will get you there. Keep them focused on income-producing activities, not busywork.

- **Identify What to Cut or Outsource**
  Make a list of tasks you can eliminate or delegate during beast mode, ex: grocery shopping, cleaning, or errands that eat into your prime work time.

- **Protect Family Connection**
  Learn the love languages of your spouse, kids, or key relationships. Schedule intentional time to love them in ways that fill their cups so they feel supported, not sidelined.

- **Double Down on Self-Care**
  When you increase your output, increase your input. Prioritize sleep, water, movement, and healthy meals to maintain energy and avoid burnout.

- **Build Systems for Sustainability**
  Set up tools, processes, and leadership so your business can run without you. Test it by stepping back for a day or two and tweak what is necessary.

- **Review and Repeat**
  After each push period, assess what worked and what didn't. Keep the wins, tweak the rest, and prepare for your next intentional sprint.

"Don't judge each day by the harvest you reap but by the seeds that you plant."

– Robert Louis Stevenson

SEBASTIAN CORDES

Accolades

- 12 years of experience in the network marketing profession

- Second-generation network marketing leader

- Built teams and customer networks across more than 30 countries

- Six-figure income earner who started while finishing a Master's in Business Development

- Featured speaker at Success Summit 3 with Frazer and Rob

- Passionate about helping families escape the 9-to-5 trap and build real freedom

THE ULTIMATE GUIDE TO CREATING A LASTING, MULTI-GENERATIONAL NETWORK MARKETING EMPIRE

What if your family could leave the nine-to-five routine behind and build something that lasts for generations? I ask this not as an abstract idea but as someone who has lived the answer. I grew up watching my mother build a network marketing business from our kitchen table. At the time, I thought it was just my "crazy mum" doing business. When I was finishing my Master's degree in business development, she invited me to join her. I stepped in, not knowing that this decision would allow me to create a life where work fits around family, instead of the other way around.

Today, more than a decade later, I'm 37 years old, a husband, a father, and a six-figure earner with teams and customers across more than 30 countries. What follows is our story of building a multigenerational network marketing business.

I personally started from zero. At first, I helped my mother between lectures and study sessions. I learned that network marketing is not like a traditional job. You set your own hours and can work from home or anywhere else that suits you. If you build it right, it can even pay you when you aren't working because of residual income. These qualities matter when you have a family. They mean you can be present for the people you love while still earning a living. But it takes time, belief, and effort. In the early days, we held home meetings, visited customers, shared products, and followed up in our free time. The flexibility allowed me to finish my studies while still supporting the leaders in our downline.

Coach's Notes – Rob & Frazer
 This is the right framing for legacy. Sebastian sets the vision early: family first, systems second, and income that outlives your calendar. It edifies the profession without sugarcoating the work.

The turning point for us came in 2013. My mum invited my brother, sister, and me to a big company event in Miami. We had only been to the United States once before, so we were excited to combine business with a holiday. Around our kitchen table in Germany, we all said, "Yes, we're in!" On stage in Miami, I saw former CEOs, engineers, teachers, and parents who had built their own network marketing businesses. They all spoke about freedom. Listening to them, I realised my mother wasn't the only one who saw the value in this model. These were professionals who had studied the same subjects I was studying. They had left comfortable careers because they wanted control over their time. We spent the week learning, celebrating, and dreaming together. On the flight home, my mother and I made a pact to work as a team. We would use our different strengths to build something bigger than any of us could do alone.

From that moment, we ran our business as a family business. We held planning sessions over dinner. We took turns presenting, ordering products, and helping new team members. We created systems for duplication. Because network marketing lets you choose your schedule and work around school or sports, our family members could participate without missing out on their own lives. They learned about goal setting and responsibility while we benefited from their fresh ideas and digital skills. Dinner conversations shifted from complaints about bosses to brainstorming sessions: who might enjoy the products, how to host fun events, and how to reach the right people for our business. Working together meant that when one of us felt discouraged, the others could offer support.

Still, we were aware that network marketing is often misunderstood. Some people see it as a secret side job or confuse it with illegal schemes. As you all know, the truth is that it's not a get-rich-quick scheme, and not everyone makes a lot of money. Some companies focus too much on recruiting and neglect real product sales. Without a clear mission and ethical leadership, people can get discouraged and quit. Knowing this, we decided to treat our business like a proper business. We chose a company with products we loved that emphasized selling over recruiting. We invested in personal growth and learned from mentors. We built a culture of honesty and service so the next generation would be proud to continue it.

Coach's Notes – Rob & Frazer
Great call-out. Values plus product-first focus is what survives cross-generationally. If you want your kids to inherit the business, build something they can be proud to wear on their jersey.

Our commitment to learning took us to many training events. One of the most important was Success Summit by Frazer Brookes, a generic training event in the United Kingdom. Thousands of distributors from many companies gathered to hear from experts. Speaking on stage alongside leaders I admired was humbling and energizing. One man shared that he missed his child's first steps because he was stuck at work; that moment pushed him to take network marketing seriously. A mother told us she built her business during nap times and late at night until she matched her salary and left her job. Their stories mirrored ours.

The big lesson from the summit was that parents want time with their children, and that network marketing can provide it if approached ethically and strategically. Speakers reminded us to focus on personal development and building leadership skills. They taught us that duplication, teaching others to do what we do, is key to creating income that doesn't depend only on our efforts. They also emphasized values that cross generations, like integrity, respect, and service.

The summit also highlighted common misconceptions. Many newcomers assume they will make a full-time income quickly. The reality is different. In the beginning, you do a lot of a little. Without proper training and clear values, people can become frustrated. Another challenge is generational conflict: younger distributors use social media easily, while older ones prefer face-to-face conversations. If we refuse to learn from each other, our business can get stuck. To avoid these traps, we encouraged our older and younger members to share skills. We didn't pressure friends to buy or stockpile products; instead, we focused on building a loyal customer base and providing value. We accepted that replacing a family salary 100 percent could take years. But we also knew that once the team was strong and independent, residual income would keep flowing even when we took time off.

As our business grew, life changed in other ways too. When my wife and I welcomed our first son, network marketing gave us something priceless: we didn't have to choose between earning money and being there for him. In the first year, I often carried Luca in a baby carrier during morning walks. When he slept, I answered messages, coached my team, and followed up with customers. Because we had built independent leaders, our income continued even when I wasn't working eight to ten hours a day. Working from home saved travel time and let me fit chores between calls. With less time, I became more focused on essential activities: sharing products, following up, and supporting my team. I could plan my day around my family's needs rather than around a boss's schedule. Walking through the neighborhood with my son strapped to my chest, I felt grateful. I saw his first smiles and heard his first sounds. In the evenings, after dinner and bath time, I spoke with team members or new prospects. Those calls weren't just about sales; they were about helping others find the same freedom. Our team's success made our family's future secure.

Becoming a parent also taught me that network marketing requires preparation. Some parents join expecting passive income right away and are disappointed when they don't get it. Without a stable customer base or strong leaders, income can drop when you work less. Fatigue and time pressure can cause new parents to skip important tasks. Others think the business will run itself and forget the years of groundwork needed. A few even push products too aggressively when they need money, damaging relationships. To enjoy time freedom during parenthood, we learned to prepare well in advance. We built duplicable systems so our team knew what to do when we were busy. We trained leaders to make decisions on their own. We used technology like video calls to stay connected without leaving home. We divided tasks at home. Above all, we treated our business as a long-term project. The work I did before having children paid off when my son Luca arrived.

Coach's Notes – Rob & Frazer
This is the blueprint young families need. Build leadership and systems before the baby arrives, not after. Preparation turns time freedom from a slogan into reality.

Looking back, three pillars made our family business possible. First, we involved everyone. When more than one family member believes in the vision and takes action, momentum multiplies. Our dinner table became our planning hub. Second, we kept learning from mentors and events. These gatherings reminded us of the importance of values, skills, and ethical practices. Third, we prepared for life's big moments. By building strong teams and duplicable systems before my son was born, we could enjoy his first year without financial stress.

This journey has not been easy. Most people in network marketing earn little or nothing, and building a large, active team takes patience and dedication. We focus on a truly impactful product and commit to steady growth. We adopted lessons from successful family businesses:

have a clear mission, involve future leaders, mentor others, celebrate wins, and stay flexible.

Our story shows that a family-run network marketing business is not just a dream. When you bring loved ones into the business, learn from others, and plan for the future, you can build income, and pass on values and skills to the next generation. The true reward isn't just money; it's a legacy of freedom, teamwork, and purpose.

If you're considering this path, start by sharing your goals with your family. Invite them to an international event and begin taking consistent steps together. With time, belief, and effort, you too can build something that lasts.

Action Items: Practical Steps for Your Family Business

1. **Set a shared vision.** Talk as a family about what you want, whether time freedom, financial security, or something else. Write down your "why."

2. **Choose the right company.** Pick a company with products you truly love.

3. **Share roles.** Use each family member's strengths, whether social media, organizing, or customer care.

4. **Learn together.** Attend events and trainings. Invest in personal growth and leadership skills.

5. **Focus on customers first.** Build trust. Offer value. Do not pressure people. Aim to serve, not sell.

6. **Create simple systems.** Set up easy-to-follow steps for product sharing, events, and team onboarding.

7. **Plan ahead for life changes.** Prepare for busy seasons like parenthood by building leaders and systems early.

8. **Keep expectations realistic.** Success takes time. Celebrate small wins and stay consistent.

9. **Lead with values.** Integrity, respect, and people-first thinking build long-term trust and results.

"Network Marketing works 100% of the time for 100% of people who give it time."

– Frazer Brookes

IMOLA-FLÓRA PUSKÁS

Accolades

- High-retention team built on connection and community in 10+ countries

- Trainer with company, hosting events and supporting new leaders

- Passionate about helping everyday people create extraordinary travel memories and a freedom lifestyle

- Committed to mastering the profession at the highest level

- On a mission to make network marketing respected, magnetic, and impossible to ignore

THE GROWTH IS THE GOAL: HOW I BECAME THE LEADER I WASN'T BORN TO BE

Topic: perseverance, self-leadership, consistent action, progress over perfection

Have you ever hit that point where you just cannot go back to Loserland anymore, but you are still not in Successland? The most frustrating place. Seeing both worlds, but not living in either. That was me.

We had just finished the first day of an event in a foreign country. My boyfriend and I went to the bus stop, but the bus had already stopped running. We had 20 euros between us. We could not afford to get a cab, so we walked. Eight kilometres every single night through dark foreign streets, but we were still the first ones to arrive the next morning.

I knew the feeling of not having enough. We did not have much financially, but what my parents lacked in money, they made up for in love and mindset. They made me feel I could achieve anything. They never pushed their views. They supported me, cheered for me, and helped in every way they could.

I thought I had found my path when I started studying software engineering. I had the plan: degree, career, stability. Fortunately, the universe had so much more planned for me.

In my first year of university, I joined network marketing. At first, I did not even know it was network marketing.

Today, I live on the beach. I work from anywhere. I travel almost every other month and visit destinations I never even dared to dream about. I help people create extraordinary memories and an extra income.

For the first time in my life, I feel I am truly contributing, serving a higher purpose. I have never felt this free, happy, and aligned. My heart, mind, and soul are in sync. Network marketing did not just change my bank account, it changed my energy, my vision, and my appreciation of life itself. I know without a doubt I have found what I will do until my last breath.

I am 26 years old, and I am just getting started. My mission is simple:

- To educate people on the real benefits of this profession.

- To help ordinary people create extraordinary memories and build extraordinary businesses.

- To raise the standard in network marketing so high that it is impossible to ignore.

- To create a culture and a team so attractive, so professional, and so powerful that it redefines the way people see our industry.

Because to me, network marketing is not just business. It is life. It is culture. And yes, it is sexy.

You do not need to be a born leader. You need to become one by refusing to quit, no matter how long it takes, and by building yourself until you are stronger than your circumstances.

It is not about luck, timing, talent, or the biggest network. It is about choosing growth again and again, through transitions, disappointments, heartbreaks, struggles, doubt, and the social pressure to shrink yourself.

If you commit to real growth, you will outlast every excuse, every setback, and every single person who said you could not.

Coach's Notes – Rob & Frazer
Imola's frame is textbook leadership development.
She shifts the spotlight from talent and timing to
repetition and standards. That is where durable leaders
are forged.

I joined with the goal to make 200 euros a month. I stayed for countless reasons, but early success was not one. I stayed for the progress, the community, and the person I was becoming. But I would be lying if I said I did not struggle with self-belief. I would set bold goals, then shrink them quietly. I would call it "strategizing," but really I was avoiding the work. I was more scared of being successful than I was of failing. The real objections you have to handle come from your own head.

One thing my mentor always showed me: leadership is not who you are when it is easy. It is who you keep becoming when it is not.

The turning point came at the same event where we walked every night. I heard something I have never forgotten: "Pay attention. Get excited. Never quit." Never forget, what feels obvious to you can be a life-changing bingo moment for someone else.

That night, I made a promise to myself: I will succeed, no matter what, no matter how long it takes, and no matter what it takes. Most people say "whatever it takes" until it actually takes something. For me, "whatever it takes" meant missing weddings, borrowing money for events and flights and trainings, or translating events even when I did not have a team.

The company I started with was in travel. I loved it from the start: the mission, the energy, the people. But then the pandemic hit, and the company had to make hard decisions. For a while, it felt like swimming upstream. Not everyone stayed. I respected their decisions, but it still hurt.

Now, let me ask you, what does "whatever it takes" look like for you? Not in theory, but in your daily choices. What are you pretending is out of your control that is actually in your power? Where are you playing small? What are you avoiding? How could you step up for your team and for the company? We always know so clearly what our mentors and company could do for us, but what can YOU do for them?

The leaders who stayed stood the test of time and loyalty. They did not flinch when it got hard, they rose. When we finally reached a fresh start with new systems and new energy, I felt that gut-level certainty, the lump in my throat, the fire in my heart. That unshakable belief. I knew I was exactly where I was meant to be, and with the right people.

These words got me through all: pay attention, get excited, never quit.

One of the first things I learned in programming is loops. They run over and over until a condition is met. Success works the same way: repeat the right actions until your goal becomes reality. Like:

while (vision > current reality):

    do consistent action;

Or even better:

while (mission not complete):

    do (learn; apply;)

Following the plan was easy because I knew if I kept repeating this loop, success was inevitable.

When you rent a café for a presentation and no one shows up, not even the team. When the Zoom is empty. People make memes of you building your dream life. How do you push through the feelings? How long does it take for you to get up after a punch? What are you telling yourself?

What I did was turn my environment into a constant reminder. All over the house I taped bingo moments, mentor quotes, vision boards, rules, strategies, and checklists. Anywhere I look I see my mission.

And I always kept my promise to myself. Quitting is not an option. I left behind friends. I borrowed money. I did whatever I could to spend time with the leaders. I walked 8 kilometres if I had to, but I never negotiated the price of success.

Ask yourself every night: did I show up today as a leader? Do you have kids? Did you fight for a better future for them? Are you closer to retiring your parents? What if your team saw you today? What if your mentor saw you today? Would they pay more attention to you, or less?

Many times I saw people coming in hot, creating massive stories in the blink of an eye. Compared to them I was barely crawling. But here is what I have learned: if you have been here for a while, use that. Stop comparing. Your progression is your superpower. It shows resilience. It shows strength and proof you are here for the long game.

Progression is inspiration. So do not ever beat yourself up if it takes more time. My first live was under 1 minute. Facebook would not let me save it because it was too short. I could have sworn it was 8 minutes minimum.

Many people do not DM me because of the company, the product, or the business. They DM me because they saw my videos when I was reading from a paper with a shaky voice, and they now see how aligned I am. It was not the perfect video that inspired them, it was the messy one. Your story is happening now. Do not rob your future team of seeing your becoming.

Coach's Notes – Rob & Frazer
This is a masterclass in public growth. Leaders who document the messy middle create permission for others. Progress beats polish for duplication every time.

When you feel stuck, ask yourself instead, "What am I avoiding that would move me forward? What am I not honouring? What should I do more of, and where do I waste my time?"

This is what I know. You do not need to wait for anything. You need to recommit. Because it works 100% of the time for 100% of the people who give it the time.

That is the truth.

You want to lead? Then lead yourself first.

You want to win? Then pay the price before you enjoy the prize.

You want to change your life? Then this is your moment.

Start right now.

Start messy, because no one ever starts perfect.

Fear will show up, but courage means moving anyway. Ask yourself, "What would I do if I knew, without a shadow of a doubt, that I could not fail?"

Loneliness will show up, but leaders walk first so others know the path exists.

The details do not matter. What matters is that you begin.

Let your pain shape your power.
Let your story become someone else's permission.

Let your grit be your brand.
Let your legacy begin now.

Because growth is not just the goal. It is the path.

Here is the part I am always looking for in books: so what do I do next? Let me share some things that helped me:

My mentor taught me that if you want to win big, you have to be a ninja in every skill. This will help you spot the weak spots, attack them, and turn them into strengths.

1. Confidence system:

Write down the 7 core skills. Which of these skills do you feel most confident in right now? Which one do you avoid? Where do you procrastinate?

Give yourself an honest score for each from 1 to 10.

Pick your lowest score and commit to improving it over the next two weeks. Read, role-play, practice, get feedback.

On the 1st and 16th of every month, go through the list and re-grade.

Repeat. When you are confident in everything, you do not procrastinate.

2. Environment system:

Your environment is either pushing you forward or pulling you back. You can turn your space into a 24/7 reminder of your mission.

Define your anchors: what lights you on fire, what inspires you? Bingo moments, reminders, goals, mantras, quotes, lessons from your mentors.

Print them out or write them down and tape them all over your home. Even fill your phone with them. Ask yourself: if a stranger walked into your home, would they think that you are mad? If not, tape more.

Refresh often. Do not let it become background noise. If you lie in bed and the reminder on the wall does not get you out of it, it must be replaced.

This way, your environment becomes a silent accountability partner, pulling you forward even on tough days.

3. Mindset builders, a.k.a. the bounce-back system:

Everyone gets punched in this business. Prospects ghost you, events flop, friends laugh, team members quit. You cannot avoid setbacks.

Daily mental fuel: feed your brain more than your doubts. The outer world follows the inner world.

10–20 minutes of a book.

A podcast episode or training.

One new idea written down daily.

Events rewire your belief faster than anything else. They make your doubts shrink and your vision expand. They are non-negotiable. I hope you have your next company event booked. If not, you know what to do.

Accountability partner: find someone who tells you the truth, not what you want to hear.

Move your body, shift your state: when negativity hits, do not sit in it. Move. Exercise, walk, dance, stretch. Physical energy unlocks mental resilience.

The bounce-back rule: never let a bad moment turn into a bad day. Do not go to bed without a win, even if it is just an appointment.

You can never avoid challenges, but you will recover faster than anyone else. That speed is what keeps you in the game long enough to win.

Get moving. Do not wait. Leaders do not wait for motivation; they take action until it appears.

Coach's Notes – Rob & Frazer
Love the systems. This turns inspiration into behaviour. Score your skills, wire your environment, and protect your bounce-back speed. That is how you stay in the game long enough to win.

Action Items

- **Recommit to growth daily.** Choose progress over perfection and keep your promise to yourself.

- **Define "whatever it takes" in behaviours.** List the uncomfortable actions you will do this week.

- **Run the loop.** Learn, apply, repeat until your goal replaces your current reality.

- **Engineer your space.** Tape up anchors, quotes, and goals. Refresh them often.

- **Book the next event.** Protect belief by putting the next training on your calendar now.

- **Adopt the bounce-back rule.** Never end the day without a win, even a small one.

"If you love life, don't waste time, because time is what life is made of."

– Benjamin Franklin

ELINA CARBLOM

Accolades

- Top leader with a thriving global team operating across 5 continents

- Qualified for every global incentive trip since 2018

- Top recruiter every year for nearly a decade

- Certified nutritionist turned freedom mentor

- Committed to impacting 1 million children through test-based health and purpose

HOW LEADING WITH PURPOSE CAN TRANSFORM LIVES – STARTING WITH YOUR OWN

The Ripple Effect – Becoming a Hero in Someone Else's Life

It was the autumn of 2015. The trees were glowing red and yellow, and the air was crisp enough to bite at your cheeks. That morning, the kids happily ran into preschool, eager to see their friends.

As always, I waved up at the window where my twins stood tapping on the glass to get my attention. Their big brother, Loe, was already inside somewhere, fully immersed in play as usual. I smiled and waved back, feeling warmth spread through my chest at the sight of their joy.

Then I got into the car to drive to work, turned on the radio, and heard the words that made my world stop.

"A father of several children has died in a construction accident."

My pulse skyrocketed. What if it was Johan...? How on earth would we survive?!

I fumbled for my phone, dialed his number. The ringing tone stretched endlessly...

Coach's Notes – Rob & Frazer
This is how purpose is born. It is rarely a motivational seminar. It is a life moment that shakes you to the core. Elina takes us right into the moment her "why" became non-negotiable.

The Years Before: Why I Started

My husband and I had already endured years of pressure and stress that felt like it was tearing us apart.

Four years earlier, the best thing in my life had happened – I became a mother for the first time.

I cherished every moment with little Loe. I remember laughing with him, feeling so proud of the happy little guy who had entered our lives. We created so many precious memories in those early days, and I thought: This is it. This is life.

But it didn't take long for life to flip upside down. I found out I was pregnant again – and this time, it wasn't just one baby, it was two. Loe's twin brothers were born only thirteen months after him.

When we came home from the hospital, nothing was the same. Loe got his mom back physically – but I wasn't really there anymore.

I was hit by postpartum depression that held me in its icy grip for three long years.

I felt no joy. No energy. Just a heavy anxiety that never let go. It was like the light in me had gone out, and the worst part was... this wasn't me. I didn't recognize myself at all.

And my mental state pulled us into financial rock bottom.

We were barely making ends meet. Living paycheck to paycheck. If something broke at home, we had to borrow money to fix it. Even my granddad had to help us financially sometimes, and I remember sitting there thinking:

I'm thirty years old. How the hell did I end up here?

I had always pictured my kids having a childhood like mine. My mom was always there – during school breaks, in the mornings, when someone forgot their gym bag, or just needed to talk.

I wanted to give my kids that same security. But how could we make it work financially? And how would we survive if something happened to Johan?

I had already been searching for new possibilities. I had been looking high and low for another way to make money without taking a regular job.

I had even come across Network Marketing before. But every time I heard the words, I thought, No, that's too salesy. Too pushy. That's not for me.

But that day in the car changed everything. With the radio blaring in the background and panic rising at the thought of losing Johan, I realized I was stuck. I had no options – but I did have a friend who had succeeded in Network Marketing and who I had been buying products from.

The Decision & The Start

That evening, I picked up my phone again. This time, my hands didn't shake.

I called my friend who had helped me with my health and said:

"Show me how to do this. I need to get unstuck."

She didn't hesitate.

"Great. We'll start tonight."

There was nothing magical about the beginning. No fireworks, no big money overnight.

I started like everyone else – baby steps. Afraid of being pushy. Afraid of failing. But also afraid of losing even more time with my kids and my life.

The spark was back.

I set my first goal: $600 per month after taxes. That was all I needed to quit my part-time job and be home with the kids more. That was all I dared to dream at the time.

I sold a few products here and there. Talked to people. Listened to their stories. And slowly, I began to understand that this wasn't about me. It was about them.

Coach's Notes – Rob & Frazer
Notice the simplicity. Elina's first dream wasn't millionaire status. It was $600. Leaders, remember: your big goals might inspire, but small achievable goals build belief.

When I Got My Time Back – And Saw My Son

When I stopped stressing just to keep life together, I truly saw my kids. For real.

I saw how Loe struggled in school. How he always stood out, always questioned things, always refused to just fit in. And how they tried to push him down, force him into a mold that was never his.

He was more and more given the role of "the black sheep." Too loud. Too wild. Too sensitive. He became the boy who was always blamed – even when he wasn't there.

But he was also the boy who stepped in when his friend was kicked on the playground while everyone else just watched. The boy whose friend's mom called me that evening to thank me because my son had the courage to act.

When I got my time back, I also got the chance to be there for my kids – the way my mom had been for me.

That's what I want to give to others. But when you're stuck in the hamster wheel, you don't always see it yourself. You think you're in control... until you wake up.

The Ripple Effect

Over time, my business grew.

Step by step, I regained my strength. Step by step, I realized this was about something much bigger than just earning $600 a month.

I started coaching my team with the same eyes I looked at Loe with. See the person – not just the results. See strengths where others only see weaknesses. Hold their vision until they can carry it themselves.

Nine years after I made my decision, Loe stood in the kitchen, looking at me with absolute certainty:

"Mom, can I come with you to the next event?"

I hesitated. The event was four full days, in English, from morning to evening.

"Don't you think that might be too much, honey? We could start with a one-day Swedish event in January instead..."

He shook his head and smiled.

"No, I think this is the perfect opportunity for me to practice."

So he packed his little suit, and we drove off.

I remember him sitting there, front row, day after day. Calm. Focused. Soaking it all in.

I also remember him glancing at me, embarrassed, when I stood up and whistled loudly during one of the talks.

"Mom... sit down..."

I just smiled and said:

"Here, you get to be yourself – exactly as you are."

And on the final evening, we were backstage when one of the company's founders walked into the room.

It was a man Loe had heard me talk about and listened to almost his entire life – but had never met.

I saw him freeze a little. He hesitated, nervous.

"Aren't you going to go say hi?" I whispered.

He looked at me. Thought for a moment. Then he gathered his courage, walked over, extended his hand, met his eyes, and introduced himself.

I felt a lump in my throat and tears burning behind my eyes as I watched him stand there – straight-backed, confident, certain.

He understood.

He understood why I had fought all these years.

It was about him. It was about us. It was about making sure no one has to shrink to fit in.

And I understood.

You never really know why you start – but one day, you understand why you keep going.

Coach's Notes – Rob & Frazer
This is legacy in motion. Elina didn't just buy time; she transferred belief. That moment with Loe proves what this business is really about: creating leaders inside your own home.

Action Steps

- **Start with their WHY.** Ask what they hope this will give them in three years. Write it down. Hold it for them when they forget.

- **Build real connection.** Every registration is a human being with a story. Call them. Listen. Send a personal message.

- **Empower their uniqueness.** See strengths where others see weaknesses. Speak life into them.

- **Lead with vulnerability.** Share your story, even the parts that feel uncomfortable. Vulnerability builds trust.

- **Keep moving forward.** Someone out there needs you to be the hero in their story.

Imagine what you could do,
if you knew you could not fail?

— Eleanor Roosevelt (Tony Robbins)

LESLIE HOCKER

Accolades

- Named one of John Maxwell's Top 1000 Influential Global Leaders

- Legendary Leader Award recipient & Board Member of the Association of Network Marketing Professionals (ANMP)

- Million Dollar Hall of Fame Member

- Built and mentored global teams across four continents, generating hundreds of millions in sales

- Former petroleum industry executive and youngest female leader in her division

THE INNER GAME OF SUCCESS: COACHING YOURSELF TO CONFIDENCE IN NETWORK MARKETING

I was 14 years old, standing behind the blocks at the Junior Olympics, knowing it was just me and the water now.

"You've got this, Leslie. Swim your own race."
That's what I whispered to myself before the horn blew. No coach on deck. Just my own voice and my decision to trust it!

From Athlete to Entrepreneur

At 14, I had qualified for the Junior Olympics in the 200-meter backstroke. The event was hundreds of miles away from my home, my coach couldn't be there that day due to a conflict, so it was just me and my mom. No coach to give me last-minute cues. No coach to remind me to swim my race. But my ever empowering and inspiring mother reminded me that I had trained for this moment. That I knew what to do. That I had practiced for this moment over and over and that I knew my strength was in my ability to finish strong. That meant I had to pace myself early and resist the urge to expend all of my energy in the first lap, because I was racing the swimmer in the next lane instead of swimming my own race.

As I stood at the edge of the pool, I coached myself with the power of my own voice. "Leslie, focus. You've trained for this. Swim your race." All the things my coach would have said to me. I hit the water and stayed calm. When I made the final turn, I gave it everything I had. And I finished strong.

That moment stuck with me. Not just because of the race, but because it was the first time I experienced the power of *coaching yourself.* The ability to tap into your inner belief system and lead from within became my foundation. Speaking to yourself as your own mentor is a skill that would carry me through becoming one of the youngest female executives in the petroleum industry and later through decades of entrepreneurship navigating success, setbacks, comebacks, and in building global teams.

Coach's Notes – Rob & Frazer
This story is such a strong opener. You show that confidence isn't about hype, it's about preparation and trust in yourself. The link you make between athletics and entrepreneurship is exactly the kind of bridge that inspires belief in others.

The Hidden Problem in Network Marketing

When I entered the world of network marketing, I quickly realized that most people weren't failing because they lacked desire. They were failing because they didn't know how to lead themselves. They came from jobs where they were managed, not mentored. So, when they join this profession, they tend to repeat the only thing they know, being an employee, and then trying to manage others instead of empowering themselves and their teams.

I watched talented people talk themselves out of opportunities before they even got started. I could see the hesitation in their posture, and hear the doubt in their voice. And I recognized it, because I'd been there. I knew what it felt like to second-guess myself, to try and "push through" by working harder instead of coaching myself with clarity and compassion.

People didn't need more tools. They needed more belief. They needed more confidence in themselves.

Coach Yourself Like a Champion

My shift came when I stopped speaking to myself like a critic and started speaking like a coach. Not hype. Not fluff. Just grounded, confident direction. I started saying things like, "Leslie, you've done the work. Let's go," or "You've done harder things than this." This wasn't toxic positivity. It was training my inner voice to be the kind of mentor I would want to follow.

One of the most powerful tools I use "and now teach others" is third-person self-talk or third-person coaching. It may sound odd at first, but research shows that using your own name when talking to yourself creates distance between your emotions and your actions. You simply speak to yourself like someone you believe in. Speak to yourself how you would want to be coached, instead of berating yourself, be kind.

As an example, instead of "I can't do this," say, "Leslie, you can do this." Instead of "I'm overwhelmed," say, "Leslie, take a breath. What's the next best step?" Using your own name creates the mental distance that helps you regulate emotion, closes the door on negative self-talk and helps you regain focus faster. It's a small shift that creates distance between you and your emotion in the moment. It helps you step out of the swirl of self-doubt and into action with clarity.

I was mentoring a rising leader, "Sara," who was brilliant but constantly consumed by doubt. Before every live video, she would tell herself: "What if I sound dumb? What if I mess up the script?" Her inner dialogue was heavy, loud, and judgmental. It stole her joy and made every public moment feel risky.

We worked together using this three-step shift:

- Pause and Notice: She would catch her negative thoughts in the moment. For example, "I'm going to mess this up."

- Name the Thought & Neutralize: She would say out loud, "Sara, you've prepared for this live, you got this!"

- Coach Forward: Then she'd use a positive coach-voice statement: "Sara, you've got value to deliver. Let's focus on one key message, then go from there."

After two weeks of practicing this, Sara's confidence in her videos jumped. Her viewers told her she seemed calmer. She made fewer mistakes (or at least didn't notice them), and she began enjoying going live.

Coach's Notes – Rob & Frazer
Your practical three-step method here is gold. It shows people how to interrupt the spiral and reset fast. A great way to think of this is as "self-duplication." If you can duplicate belief in yourself, you're far more effective at teaching others to believe in themselves too.

How to Shift Your Inner Game (3-Step Framework)

- Notice the Narrative
  Pay attention to how you're speaking to yourself. Is it fear-based? Shame-based? Would you talk to a teammate the way you're talking to yourself?

- Name and Neutralize
  When you hear inner criticism, pause. Say your name. Interrupt the spiral. Example: "Leslie, you're not failing. You're learning." Reframe without ignoring reality.

- Coach Yourself Forward
  End with direction: "Leslie, here's what we're going to do next." Clarity builds confidence. Your voice becomes your strategy.

I use the third-person coaching technique before big presentations, during team launches, or even in quiet moments of uncertainty. You don't need a motivational speech. You need a coach in your corner – and that starts with being one for yourself.

Self-coaching works when it becomes your default voice. Practicing reframes daily, builds resilience and most importantly rewires your response to challenge.

The Two Prongs of Real Empowerment Coaching

As my business partner and husband, Ron Forrester, and I built organizations across North America, Latin America, Europe, and Asia, we saw that duplication didn't just happen because of systems. It happened because people felt seen, heard, and empowered. And that always starts with the relationship we have with ourselves and how we coach ourselves. This is why constant personal development is so key for long-term success.

There are two key prongs to real coaching in network marketing. The first is helping someone connect with why they started this journey. But I don't just ask people, "What's your why?" That question is too vague for most people to answer. Instead, I ask, "What is it that you have ever wanted to Do, to Be, or to Have? Answer this as if money and time are no obstacle." That question gets them dreaming again. Once we know that, we can reverse-engineer a plan that feels personal, energizing, and sustainable.

The second prong is the process I call "Tell, Show, Try, Do." First, we tell them (train them). Then we show them how through modeling the activity or action ourselves. Then they try it while we observe and offer feedback. Finally, they do it on their own. That's how real confidence is built. When they actually experience their own win or wins. And our job, as leaders, is to create an environment where they feel safe enough to try.

Coach's Notes – Rob & Frazer
Your "Tell, Show, Try, Do" framework is a classic leadership multiplier. It's also a reminder for leaders not to shortcut the process. Duplication happens when people get real wins themselves, not when they just watch someone else succeed.

Vision: Empowered Leadership Starts With You

When you coach yourself with belief, clarity, and grace, it's contagious. You show others what it looks like to rise without beating yourself up and how to grow without hustling for worth. You become the kind of leader people feel safe around, because you've done the inner work.

And when enough of us do that, we raise the standard of leadership in this profession. We stop managing people and start mentoring them. We stop fixing and start empowering. And that ripple creates teams that are not only productive, but fulfilled.

The Solution: Create Inner Safety

People don't grow when they feel judged. They grow when they feel safe. Safe to try. Safe to fail. Safe to be new. And the same goes for us, as leaders. If you want to create that environment for others, you have to create it for yourself first.

That's why I always return to the principle: coach yourself like you would coach your best team member. Encourage yourself. Acknowledge progress. Focus on your progress and your wins, no matter how small, not perfection. This is the mindset that keeps you in the game long enough to reach your goal(s).

"Masters treat their business like a game worth playing!
Since we all have a next level and there is no finish line, keep playing!"
~Leslie Hocker

Action Steps

For Yourself:

- Practice coaching yourself in third person.

- Say your name out loud when you feel doubt: "Leslie, you've got this. Let's focus."

- Create a "Self-Coaching Toolkit" on your phone or desk: go-to phrases, affirmations, reminders.

- Journal at night: "When did I coach myself well today? Where can I improve?"

For Your Team:

- Before coaching, compliment on something they did right.

- Then ask, "Do I have permission to coach you?"

- Or ask, "May I give you some tips that could help you be better and grow faster?"

- Always coach in a way that uplifts, not diminishes.

For Momentum:

- Review your dream goal daily

- Evaluate performance based on your minimum goal

- Celebrate your stretch efforts – even if they don't reach the dream (yet)

Final Words

Remember, none of us are born with confidence. Confidence is a learned skill. Like any skill, it takes time and is developed with daily practice... one powerful thought and action at a time.

"With every heartbeat you have one less heartbeat to love, one less heartbeat to succeed."

— Tim Grover

SUE WILLIAMS

Accolades

- Ranked up three times

- Developed a team across the UK, with plans to expand into Dubai and USA

- Renowned for leadership skills in end-of-life care and dementia care

- Employed and led a team of over 100 staff

- Recently qualified as a certified life coach

HOW TO CHANGE DIRECTION AND RECLAIM YOUR INNER POWER: IT'S NEVER TOO LATE TO START AGAIN

"When the Dust Settles"

When the dust is settling, there's no applause, just silence, pain, and the realisation that you survived something that was meant to break you.

For 32 years, I was a nurse, an end-of-life nurse. I held the hands of people who were taking their final breaths, whispering comfort into the darkest hours. I built relationships with them and their loved ones, based on trust, compassion, kindness, and understanding.

I dedicated my time and efforts into making sure that those final weeks or months were comfortable, and when the time came for them to leave this world, they left with grace, dignity, and peace.

My career wasn't just what I did. It was who I was. I had given it everything I had. It was me. I was it.

During the last 10 years of my career, I took derelict buildings and created a care facility that was graded as excellent. Everyone told me that I was being ridiculous but I had the vision of what it was going to be. It was once described as "home from home, where love greets you at the door and is found in every corner." Exactly my vision.

I had led the way in developing something special, and I spent every day of those 10 years making sure that those people had the best of everything, and most importantly, the right to be themselves.

And suddenly, it stopped.

Ill health took it from me, and I was left with a version of myself that I didn't recognise. I had lost a version that I didn't know how to live without.

For 6 years, I had ignored a health condition — Ischemic Heart Disease. I had hidden the symptoms from family and friends, and became an expert in sitting down when I could feel the pain in my chest, putting a smile on my face and assuring everyone that I was okay. Why? Because there was always someone who had needs that were greater than mine. Always a hand to hold, always a family to support and console. At least that's what I told myself.

In 2021 my body decided enough was enough, and I was told that I needed cardiac surgery.

In an extremely weakened state, I was admitted to hospital.

On that day, saying goodbye to my family and my dogs was hard and emotional. I was so weak and sick, I truly believed I had said the last goodbye. I wanted to tell them I would be watching their progress in life and just how much I loved them. I knew that would worry them so I just said, "I'll see you soon." Those words and moments still haunt me.

The surgery was more complex than anticipated, and the recovery was a lot longer. I woke up in an Intensive Care Unit, and, having heard the details of it all, I knew my career was over.

I was a leader who had now become a follower, a nurse who had become the patient, the strong one who was now weak — physically, emotionally, and psychologically.

Coach's Notes – Rob & Frazer
This is such a raw and powerful story. You don't just describe resilience, you embody it. Readers will instantly connect with the way you've taken a personal crisis and turned it into something meaningful.

What followed was 2 years of hell.

I felt that part of me had died with no time to plan my exit, no time to say goodbye. My dreams had gone too. To be perfectly honest, there were days when I wished I hadn't survived the operation. I had promised so many people that I would be there for them, and I had failed them.

Grief consumed me and I had no idea what to do next. I had a question that was on constant repeat in my head — if I'm not her anymore, then who am I?

I was in a dark, dismal place, I could see the door that I needed to open but I had no courage or desire to do that.

At some point, in those two years of crawling through the wreckage of the life I used to have, I distinctly recall hearing my mum saying, "Wait until the dust settles and then we can see the way forward." She was full of wisdom and always had the right words. So, in the silent, painful, dark world I was in, I did exactly that.

I waited for the dust to settle.

There are stages in the grieving process: denial, anger, bargaining, despair, acceptance, and hope.

Not necessarily in that order, I visited and revisited these stages so many times and finally found myself reaching acceptance and hope. This is when I opened the door and saw the first glimmer of the new dawn.

I had taken a huge step — the dust had finally settled. It was time for me to take responsibility for reshaping my future. My life.

Before I opened the door to my new life, I had gathered together what was left of my old life. The skills I had acquired — leadership, compassion, empathy, patience, understanding, the ability to listen, to know when to stay silent and when to respond. I now had to find a use for those skills.

First, I had to find an income.

I began to look for work, and came across an advert that gave me an opportunity to be my own boss and earn in the process. I repeatedly saw this and eventually enquired. Then I sat on it for a few months, my head filled with doubt and what ifs.

So much had changed during the years since Covid had forced the world into a new way of living and working. People were working from home now, technology played an even bigger part in life than it ever had before. This terrified me. I was hopeless with technology, even worse with social media. My Facebook account was void of friends and followers (my choice). The words "Instagram," "TikTok," "LinkedIn" struck fear through my entire body.

To my surprise, I found myself signing up to the advert that had repeatedly shown up. With great trepidation, I began my new journey.

ENTER NETWORK MARKETING.

If someone had told me this was my new path in life, I would have laughed. Me? In sales? I've spent my life in scrubs!

It wasn't selling that hooked me though, it was the people.

Coach's Notes – Rob & Frazer
The way you capture your transition into network marketing is so relatable. Many people start with hesitation, but your story proves that authenticity and heart are far more powerful than perfect scripts.

My daughter told me to listen to someone — I had no idea who it was, or what I was listening to, I just knew from the very first video I watched that he would give me the inspiration to use my skills in a very different way.

I was fixated on his energy, his positivity, the fact that he openly admitted he felt useless at the beginning of his journey into network marketing. He was, and is, the amazing Frazer Brookes.

I listened to everything he had to say, and I began to create something I would grow to love. It was something that I could do from home, on my terms, with the experience I already had.

And so, I started — slowly at first, hesitantly. Awful selfies, voice notes that took at least ten takes to record. I had no idea what I was doing, but I was doing it anyway!

At first it was like talking to an empty room. No one was there, no one was watching. I kept going though, because slowly but surely my efforts were bringing ME back.

As the weeks went on, something incredible happened — people began to follow me, friend requests were popping up. Not because I was using a sales pitch, but because I was being me. I was real. I had no ego to polish, but I had courage and I had a heart.

I had followed advice and acted on those words that I'm sure many of us have heard: "Strangers become friends. Friends become family."

Sure enough, strangers did become friends. They connected with a woman who had to rebuild her life, who knew pain, who had lost everything — her home, her dreams, her identity — and decided to rise again.

Before I knew it, I had a team. People who weren't looking for someone perfect. They were looking for someone to give them belief that it is okay to begin again, to try something new, to lead by example carrying the scars of the battles they had fought.

Coach's Notes – Rob & Frazer
This section is a blueprint for leading with vulnerability. You show that credibility doesn't come from being flawless — it comes from being real, rebuilding, and giving people hope. That's the type of leadership this profession needs more of.

I was using my skills helping them, cheering them on through their new path in life, giving them hope. The difference was, I was no longer wearing a uniform. I was building a business. A brand. A new life. I was giving hope to those who had none.

I have learned that leadership isn't about being the loudest or the strongest, it's about being the clearest in your "why."

This is my "why" — everyone deserves more than survival. We all deserve joy, flexibility, the right to own our own time, our own story.

Network marketing gave me all of that. It gave me a reason to get up in the morning. It gave me back me. The passionate, caring, driven woman I thought had disappeared in that Cardiac Surgery unit.

And Now?

- I lead a team that is growing.

- I have ambition to grow it in size and strength.

- I have ranked up 3 times.

- I have coached others through doubt and fear.

- I have celebrated wins with new starters.

- I've watched lives change, just as mine did.

And within this chapter I have told my story, and my voice has been heard.

I haven't spoken on stage... YET.
I haven't earned a multiple figure income... YET.

What I have done is priceless. I have lived to tell the tale, which will and has inspired lots of people.

Now... if you had told the woman in that hospital bed that she would be speaking to others about resilience and entrepreneurship, she would have laughed. Or cried. Or both.

But here is the magic.

When the dust settles, you get to rebuild. So here I am. A woman rebuilt. A nurse at heart, a leader by choice. A survivor who didn't just survive. She soared.

If any of this resonates with you, HEAR ME NOW:

You are not too old. You are not too broken. You are not too late.

You are still here, and therefore, you are not done.

I didn't think I could ever start again. But when the dust settled, I didn't just find a new life, I found myself. And I promise you, that is worth everything.

I have my dreams again.

I thank God every day that I am still here.

Looking back on that period of time, I think it's important to say that however dark the days become, there is always a new dawn coming. Never let go of that belief.

We all go through changes in our lives, we all have problems, we all hit speed bumps. The important thing is how we deal with it. There is no handbook, no map to follow, no hard and fast rules to help you overcome it. Take as much time as you need to reflect, to feel the emotions that surface, until one day, you find the courage to face life again. Remember those words: wait until the dust settles.

My journey continues, as will yours. In the meantime, consider taking these steps:

Action Steps

- Create a journal of your journey, use it to look back on, take pride in each step you take forward

- Take stock of any knowledge or skills that you have, think about how you can use them going forward

- Take time to look back on the days where you were fulfilled, happy, and successful. Remember the positivity of those times, record them, and look back on them when you feel negativity creeping in

- Tell yourself each day, "I am worthy of happiness, I will be successful, I will rebuild my life and move on, I will not let fear get in my way"

In the words of Walt Disney:
"All our dreams can come true, if we have the courage to pursue them."

"Every adversity, every failure,
every heartache carries with
it the seed of an equal
or greater benefit."

– Napoleon Hill

NATHANIEL HYDE

Accolades

- Three years in Direct Sales/Affiliate Marketing

- Built a team in over four countries

- Overturned adversity in multiple ways

- Living authentically every day

HOW TO UNLOCK YOUR WHY AND BECOME YOUR TRUE AUTHENTIC SELF

The day I almost ended my life was the day I finally started to understand it.

I saw it so clearly—my brother, kneeling in front of my nieces, trying to explain why Uncle Nathaniel wasn't coming back.

That vision didn't just stop me. It snapped something inside me awake.

We don't always notice when we begin to lose ourselves. It doesn't happen all at once. It's subtle. Quiet. It's the slow erosion of identity—piece by piece—until one day you look in the mirror and barely recognise the person staring back.

For me, it started in childhood. I was bullied throughout school. Not just the odd insult in the corridor, but sustained, targeted, and cruel bullying that chipped away at my sense of safety and self-worth. I remember the pit in my stomach walking to school, the dread that clung to me in the lunch hall, and the silence I kept—because speaking out only made it worse. I learned early that the world could be brutal, especially if you were different, sensitive, or simply not part of the crowd.

And so I adapted. I tried to blend in. I made myself smaller. I became whoever I needed to be just to get through the day. I wore masks. I made people laugh. I learned how to disappear in plain sight. I laughed off pain and buried the truth because vulnerability, in that environment, was dangerous.

What I didn't realise at the time is that when you deny parts of yourself to survive, you eventually forget who you really are.

Those coping strategies followed me into adulthood. They became hardwired. Keep the peace. Avoid conflict. Don't show weakness. Keep smiling. Make people comfortable. I told myself I was fine, even when I wasn't. And that armour—although it had protected me—also kept me from being seen, known, and truly loved. It kept me distant even from myself.

Years later, I found myself in a marriage that would further fracture me. Domestic abuse isn't always obvious from the outside. It's not just bruises or shouting matches. Sometimes, it's silence used as punishment. It's subtle manipulation. It's being made to question your reality. It's your confidence being chipped away with every comment, every eye roll, every calculated withdrawal of affection. It's the slow, steady draining of your spirit by someone who says they love you.

By then, I was already fragile—but I didn't realise how fragile until everything collapsed.

Coach's Notes – Rob & Frazer
The vulnerability you share here is courageous. You're showing people that strength isn't about having a perfect past, it's about finding clarity and resilience through struggle. That lesson will land deeply with readers.

In 2017, I was involved in a serious car accident. One of those moments where life splits into "before" and "after." What should have been a normal day became the moment that shook my nervous system to the core. I walked away physically intact—but mentally, everything changed. In the months that followed, I was diagnosed with PTSD, anxiety, and mild depression.

Everything became difficult. Noise. Crowds. Sleep. Trust. The simple act of getting out of bed some days felt like climbing a mountain barefoot. My mind was constantly on high alert. I couldn't switch off. I couldn't explain it to people in a way that made sense, and I didn't want to sound weak or broken, so I mostly stayed silent.

And so I did what I'd always done—I kept going. I wore the mask. I smiled. I made others laugh. I said I was okay.

But inside, I was unravelling.

By 2018, I hit my lowest point. The combination of long-standing emotional wounds, the trauma of the accident, and the isolation of a toxic relationship had broken me. I felt like I was existing in slow motion. I would lie in bed staring at the ceiling, unable to move, paralysed by a fog of hopelessness that made the world seem grey and meaningless.

It wasn't loud or chaotic. It was quiet. Numb. The kind of numb that feels like you're floating through life like a ghost, disconnected and exhausted. I remember that night so clearly. The moment where I genuinely believed the world would be better off without me.

And then... a single image stopped everything.

I saw my brother. Sitting my nieces down. Trying to explain why Uncle Nathaniel was gone. I imagined their little faces—confused, heartbroken, wondering why I'd left. That vision broke me in the most important way. It didn't just snap me out of the fog—it woke something up.

I couldn't do it. I couldn't leave them with that story. I couldn't let that be my legacy.

So, I stayed.

That moment—raw, terrifying, sacred—became the start of something new. It didn't fix everything overnight, but it gave me a reason. A spark. A why.

We hear a lot these days about "finding your why." It's become a buzzword, hasn't it? Something slapped on motivational posters and coffee mugs. But here's what I've learned: your real why doesn't arrive neatly packaged with a bow. It shows up in the rubble. It whispers to you in the dark when you've got nothing left. It doesn't look like inspiration—it looks like survival.

Coach's Notes – Rob & Frazer
This reframe of "finding your why" is brilliant. You take it out of cliché territory and make it real. Readers will relate because their why often comes out of hardship, not highlight reels.

My why is legacy. It's about showing my nieces and nephew what strength really looks like. Not the kind of strength that never bends or breaks—but the kind that rises, scarred and wiser. It's about turning pain into purpose. It's about standing in the mess of my past and saying, "This didn't destroy me—it defined me."

But unlocking your why is only the beginning.

So how do you do it?

How do you go from broken and lost to purposeful and aligned?

Here's the 3-step method I use—and return to—when I feel disconnected or stuck.

Step 1: Revisit the Breaking Point

Ask yourself:

What was the moment that nearly broke me—but didn't?

This is not about wallowing in the past—it's about reclaiming power from it. Your why is often born in the place where everything almost ended. That moment you chose to stay. That moment you got back up. Go back there. Not to relive the pain, but to honour your decision to fight.

Get quiet. Get honest. What hurt? What changed? What did you learn about yourself in that moment?

Write it down. Even if it's messy.

Step 2: Identify Who You're Doing It For

Ask:

Who benefits when I show up fully? Who do I refuse to give up on?

Your why becomes unstoppable when it includes others. For me, it's my nieces and nephew. They remind me daily what love looks like. Maybe for you it's your children. Your parents. Your future self. Your community. Or someone you've never even met, but who will one day need your story to find their strength.

Picture them. Name them. Feel the weight of your commitment to them.

Step 3: Build With It Daily

Ask yourself:

What decision can I make today that honours that commitment?

You don't need to build your legacy in one leap. You just need to build it intentionally. Maybe today, that's starting the conversation. Booking the therapy session. Leaving the job. Launching the business. Saying no. Saying yes. Choosing you.

Progress isn't about pace—it's about direction.

Coach's Notes – Rob & Frazer
Your 3-step framework is clear, actionable, and deeply personal. It gives the reader a repeatable process to connect with their why and apply it daily, which makes your story practical as well as inspiring.

The beauty of becoming your true, authentic self is that it gives others permission to do the same. You stop performing, and you start connecting—deeply, honestly, humanly. You build real relationships. You create real change. And you leave behind a real legacy.

Imagine waking up every day knowing that you're living in alignment with who you are, not who the world told you to be. Imagine the freedom of no longer having to fake it, to force it, or to hide it. That's what's waiting on the other side of your "why."

You don't need to be perfect to begin this journey. You just need to be honest. You just need to take one step.

If today was the day you stopped pretending, what truth would you finally speak—and who would you become? That version of you is already within reach. Write it down. Revisit it daily. Let it lead you.

You don't find your why by escaping your story—you find it by stepping into it, fully and fearlessly.

"Whether you think you can or you think you can't, you're right."
— Henry Ford

LISA GRIMOLFSON

Accolades

- 5 Figure Earner

- Champion Circle Earner

- Featured guest on Rob Sperry's Network Marketing Breakthrough Podcast

- Inducted into the Manitoba Volleyball Hall Of Fame

- Passionate about helping others see their true potential

THE COURAGE TO BE SEEN: A GUIDE FOR THE QUIET AND INSECURE

My Invisible Girl Story

Growing up, I lacked confidence in myself. I was that quiet, shy little girl who clung to her parents wherever we went. I remember sitting in the front of the grocery cart, completely panicked if my mom even took two steps away. I would reach out and pull her back to me, afraid to be alone, even for a second. I was a preschool dropout, and I cried every single day during the first few months of Kindergarten. I was so shy that I couldn't even bring myself to speak to my own aunts and uncles. At family gatherings, you'd find me curled up on my mom's or grandma's lap. If I spoke a word to anyone outside my immediate family, it was rare enough to make people stop and stare. I stayed that way until I was at least 12 years old.

Coach's Notes – Rob & Frazer
Your transparency here is powerful. So many readers will see themselves in your story and instantly feel less alone. This is the kind of vulnerability that inspires belief in others.

Micro-Moments of Courage

Junior High was when I began to change and grow. I started playing sports and making new friends. Volleyball was my sport all throughout school, and it played a huge role in my personal growth. I didn't believe I was great at sports, but I had a coach in grade 7 who changed my perspective. He was incredibly positive and uplifting. Even when I made mistakes or our team lost, he was cheering us on. He noticed skills in me before I could see them myself. Because he believed in me, I started to believe in myself and I began to work harder. Volleyball was no longer just fun, it became a part of my identity. It made me feel like I was good at something and I enjoyed doing it.

Then came a major blow. In Grade 10, I tried out for the team and I didn't make it. I was devastated. In that moment, I believed I wasn't good enough. My confidence was shattered. I thought if I wasn't good enough to make the team then, what was the point in trying again the next year? That experience shook me deeply.

Shortly after that, my parents encouraged me to get my first job. I was terrified. I still didn't feel confident in myself, let alone in talking to strangers and applying for a job. I eventually got hired as a cashier at Walmart, and I'll never forget my first shift. I was beet red, shaking, and my voice wavered every time I spoke. I hated being watched while bagging groceries, afraid I'd do something wrong. I felt like people were judging my every move, but I needed the job, so quitting wasn't an option.

Even though I was scared, I kept going. Every day I went back, I grew just a little more confident in my abilities. I learned more about the job and started to become more comfortable talking to customers each day. Slowly, I started to come out of my shell after choosing to do it scared those first few weeks. Eventually, I became a customer service manager in charge of the front end, overseeing employees and assisting customers. I even began to enjoy talking to people. That job was the foundation of my confidence, it forced me to face my fears and helped me realize that I could do hard things. It taught me that if I wanted to learn and grow as a person, I had to get out of my comfort zone and do things that scared me.

Coach's Notes – Rob & Frazer
This section shows the compounding power of courage. You make it clear that confidence doesn't come from waiting until you feel ready, it comes from action. Readers will take this as proof they can practice confidence into existence.

LEADERSHIP UNLOCKED

Confidence Comes Through Action, Not Readiness

After high school, I went to University for 7 years and I became a teacher. On my first day of my teaching practicum, I had to read a book out loud to a group of first graders. It sounds simple, but I was incredibly insecure. I had a monotone voice and I was worried the kids wouldn't pay attention. I was sweating, and my voice was shaking, my face was beet red, but I pushed through and just kept reading. I wouldn't allow myself to quit because it was uncomfortable.

The more I practiced, the more comfortable I became. Over time, I developed expression in my reading, I learned how to engage the kids, hold their attention and I began to believe in my teaching abilities. Confidence didn't show up overnight, it came through showing up and doing it scared, over and over again.

When I started to transition into network marketing, I realized I had already been preparing for it for two decades. Between customer service, sports, and teaching, I had practiced leadership, communication, and building relationships. Even so, I still had a lot to learn in the network marketing space. Reaching out to people I hadn't talked to in years was still terrifying. I didn't want to be seen as annoying or pushy, as I think most network marketers feel the same. I started to just do it scared because I knew from past experiences that growth comes from getting out of your comfort zone and failing forward. I knew that if I just started messaging people, I would learn what to say and what not to say, I would get better with each conversation.

What I eventually learned is that the way you think about it also matters. When I started to tell myself I was helping others, whether through products, community, or opportunities, I stopped feeling scared and started feeling excited. I began to treat each conversation as

142

a chance to serve. Over time, I went from chatting with one customer at a time to leading training calls and running power hours. I didn't get there by waiting until I felt "ready." I did it scared, and that made all the difference.

Coach's Notes – Rob & Frazer
The "do it scared" mindset you model here is such a strong framework. Readers will see that fear doesn't disappear, but confidence grows when you move forward anyway. That's a duplicatable skill that anyone can practice.

The Inner Dialogue Battle

There's always that voice in your head. The one that says, "You're not good enough." Sometimes, that voice doesn't even come from you, it's been passed down through the words or actions of others. Maybe a family member made you feel like you didn't measure up. Maybe it's just something you internalized over time because of a lack of feeling successful.

That voice once told me that I couldn't do things, that I would fail, or that no one liked me. So, I made excuses. I avoided the scary stuff, but eventually, I learned about positive self-talk. At first, I didn't believe any of it. When people complimented me, I wanted to deflect, but I forced myself to just say "thank you." I started repeating what others said about me until I started to believe it.

When I felt scared, I'd say, "I can do hard things." I used it everywhere, even in sports. I used to be so scared to go up to bat during a baseball game, but I'd tell myself, "I got this" and step up anyway. Over time, that turned into, "I'm going to smash this ball," and most of the time, I did.

One of my next big fears? Speaking on stage at a conference. It's a big one for me. But I'm already working on it. I picture myself doing it (visualization is a great strategy for overcoming fears), I feel the nerves and then I tell myself, "If I can speak in front of an entire school, I can speak on that stage too." When my anxiety starts to rise, I breathe, three deep breaths, in through the nose, out through the mouth. I remind myself I'm safe. That I've done hard things before. That I'm capable of doing this too. I'm preparing myself for my future and again, getting out of my comfort zone and doing scary things.

Being Seen Without Needing Validation

As I gained confidence in myself and started to love who I was, I began to try more new things. Growing up, my dad taught me how to use tools, paint, and renovate a home. I always had an interest in renovations and building things. Unfortunately, after becoming a single mom at the age of 20, I didn't have a lot of time to explore that side of myself.

About 8 years later, during a difficult time, I decided I was going to stop relying on others and I was going to build my own garden boxes. I loved gardening, but I didn't love bending over to weed. I couldn't afford to buy any, so I turned to YouTube and figured it out on my own. I was nervous to start, but I had faith that they would work out. I started by drawing up a design and then I started to get to work. I finished the first one in one day and I was so proud. That was the spark that ignited my love for DIY and building. After that, I knew I could build anything I wanted too, I just had to take the time to figure it out. I eventually renovated my very first home, built a bed frame, a kitchen table, a dog kennel, a fireplace, and more.

With each project, my pride grew. Not because others praised me (some people actually didn't want to see my accomplishments), but because I knew what I'd done. That inner pride became my validation that I am capable of doing anything I put my mind to. It's the same in my business. Whether I'm signing a new customer or just sending out one invite, or getting a new exposure, I celebrate every small win. It's proof that I'm moving forward. The more actions I take scared, the more belief I build. The courage comes from showing up, not from being seen.

Your Voice Has Value

Even now, with all I've done, I still get nervous. When I started network marketing, I was scared to reach out. I didn't want to be seen as "that girl" in people's inboxes. I was afraid of rejection. Then one of my mentors said something that changed everything: "If you believe you're helping, you won't feel like you're bothering people."

That stuck with me. And it helped me shift my perspective. Now, I don't feel like I'm selling, I feel like I'm offering something that could change someone's life, and I've seen it happen many times. Every time a customer or teammate shares their story, it reminds me that this work matters and by using my voice and offering what I have, I am able to help change one life at a time.

Negative thoughts still show up. But now, I'm equipped to handle them. I've built a foundation of belief, and I know that my voice matters. It doesn't have to be the loudest in the room. Sometimes it's the quiet, steady voices that make the biggest impact.

Tips for the Quiet and Insecure

1. **Practice Positive Self-Talk**
   Start your day by looking in the mirror and saying something kind. Tell yourself you're strong, beautiful, and capable. It feels weird at first, but over time, it works.

2. **Take One Bold Step Daily**
   Pick something that scares you, just one thing, and visualize yourself doing it successfully. Then go do it. One small step each day builds confidence over time.

3. **Let Fear Ride Shotgun, Not Drive**
   You don't have to get rid of fear. Let it be there. But remind it that you're in charge. Fear is just a signal that you're growing.

4. **Practice in Safe Spaces, Then Expand**
   Practice your new skills with someone who makes you feel safe. Then try it in front of one or two more people. Slowly stretch your comfort zone. Growth follows effort.

Final Thoughts

Confidence isn't something you're born with, it's something you build. It's in the action, in the repetition, and in the choice to show up, even when you're scared. I used to be the invisible girl, shy, unsure, and small. But through each little act of courage, I became visible. I became me.

And if I can do it, so can you.

"Success doesn't come from what you do occasionally. It comes from what you do consistently."

— Marie Forleo

LOUISE GATLAND

Accolades

- Replaced full-time income in just 3.5 months

- Built a team in the thousands

- Became a six-figure earner in under 18 months

- Spoken on stages across the UK, Europe, and USA

- Co-author of two top-selling books

BUILT IN THE QUIET: WHY THE BEST LEADERS DON'T WAIT TO BE CHOSEN

The Day Everything Changed

I didn't step into network marketing with a polished vision board and a master plan. I stepped in with a knot in my stomach and a fierce determination not to let my kids down.

I joined in July 2017, but when I lost my job in November 2017 I hit rock bottom. It was December 1st, 2017, three weeks before Christmas, when I lost my job in education. Walking out with a cardboard box, one question hit me: Now what? I had three children, bills that didn't pause for sympathy, and no appetite for telling them Christmas would be "different this year."

Even before that day I'd been treading water. My monthly pay vanished on arrival: food, bills, uniforms, bus fare. I was existing in a world designed to be lived in, and the gap between those two was swallowing me.

A few months earlier someone had mentioned a network marketing opportunity. I didn't know the language, systems, or culture. No yachts, no hype. I simply thought, Maybe this will help me generate additional income. When the job disappeared, that whisper became the only sound in the room.

January had always been the "sensible plan" — get another job. But safety can be the slowest route to the same dead end. Sitting at my kitchen table, I made a decision that still defines my life: I'm going all in. Not when it's convenient. Now.

There were no fireworks. Just a notebook, late nights, awkward first messages, shaky first presentations, and a quiet promise: I will not wait to be chosen. I will choose me.

Coach's Notes – Rob & Frazer
Your description of that turning point is incredibly relatable. Many leaders begin in the middle of crisis, and your decision to "choose yourself" is the exact model others need to see.

YouTube University and the Power of Self-Education

With no mentor and no playbook, I did what hungry people do: I searched. Into the bar I typed, "how to build a team in network marketing," and up popped a video from Frazer Brookes. It felt like someone turned the lights on — the what and the why: posture, language, daily method, belief.

I made one rule: if I learn it today, I apply it today. I sent the messages he suggested, refined the language he modelled, and when something worked, I taught it to my fledgling team. Years later I'd join his Inner Circle, but by then I had already internalised the most valuable lesson: winners don't wait for someone to hand them a plan, they build one.

Self-education birthed self-leadership. I stopped asking, When will someone show me what to do? and started asking, What can I do with what I already know? Spectators wait for perfect conditions. Builders create progress in imperfect conditions.

Leading Without Permission

Across this industry I see people waiting — for their upline, for confidence, for perfect timing. Waiting is a polite way to quit.

I didn't have perfectly aligned support at first. Eventually I connected with uplines; we didn't always agree, but I learned to observe what worked, duplicate it, and adapt it to my voice. Leadership is not unanimity. Leadership is ownership. The title arrives after the behaviour, not before it. The market pays attention to results, and results are built in the quiet.

Coach's Notes – Rob & Frazer
Your challenge to stop waiting for perfect conditions is a leadership masterclass. You remind people that leadership begins the moment they take ownership, not when someone gives them a title.

Built in the Quiet

People ask, What was the big break? There wasn't one. There were hundreds of tiny acts no one saw.

My youngest was five. I didn't have long stretches of free time — school runs, dinner, homework, real life. So I learned to work in ten- to fifteen-minute sprints. Ten minutes of focused reach-outs in the car park. Fifteen minutes of follow-ups while the pasta boiled. Two voice notes on a walk to the post box. I stacked those sprints and discovered a truth most people miss: intensity beats duration when it's applied consistently.

Quiet work looks ordinary: tracking names, reminders, three-ways, event invites, belief built one conversation at a time. But ordinary done daily compounds into extraordinary. The algorithm rewards consistency. So does life.

The Operating System: Discipline Over Drama

From day one I treated my business like a business. Systems over sporadic effort. Here's the operating system I still use.

1. **The Non-Negotiable DMO**
   Every day, regardless of moods or circumstances:

- 5–10 new connections (genuine conversation, not spam)

- Follow up every open thread (people are busy; follow-up is service)

- Show up publicly (post, story, or live — document the journey)

- One PS3: Peek interest, Show the plan, 3-way call or chat

I call it Minimum Viable Momentum — light enough for hard days, strong enough to move the needle. Consistency beats unsustainable intensity.

2. **Learn → Apply → Teach**
   Information without implementation bloats confidence and shrinks results. If a tactic is worth writing down, it's worth trying within 24 hours. Once it works, teach it. Teaching deepens mastery and multiplies impact.

3. **Track the Truth**
   I tracked names, exposures, objections, follow-up dates, invites, conversions. When feelings said I was "doing everything," data told the truth. Progress loves clarity.

4. **Momentum Windows**
   Every decision has a half-life. After a powerful call there's a two-hour window where belief is highest. That's when I stack follow-ups, book three-ways, and send tools. Miss the window, miss the momentum.

5. **The 72-Hour Rule**
   For new partners: within 72 hours they should (a) make a social post, (b) invite to a presentation, (c) get their first three-way scheduled. Fast action cements belief. Slow starts harden doubt.

Coach's Notes – Rob & Frazer
Your operating system is world-class. Especially the
concept of Minimum Viable Momentum. Leaders will
see how simple, consistent actions compound into
massive results. This section is a playbook by itself.

Resilience Over Recognition

Recognition is wonderful, but it cannot be the fuel. If you only work when people are clapping you'll stall when the room is quiet. There were months I worked hard and results lagged. Seeds don't sprout on our schedule. I kept planting.

Some people quit because they confuse silence with failure. I clapped for small wins: a booked call, a brave post, a follow-up I didn't feel like sending. Celebrating behaviour kept me moving.

Building Leaders, Not Dependents

I never wanted a team that "followed Louise." I wanted a team that followed principles. That required modelling, not just messaging.

- I showed my calendar. People don't believe advice; they believe schedules.

- I was visible at events. I didn't ask anyone to attend what I skipped.

- I shared my numbers. Transparency builds trust.

- I elevated early leaders. Stage time and responsibility are accelerators.

Culture eats tactics. Ours says: move first, own outcomes, lift as you climb, speak belief, act.

Advanced Leadership Principles

Principle 1: Duplicate What Works, Not What's Trendy
Trends entertain; systems duplicate. Guard your team from "strategy hopping." Define the core plays and run them relentlessly.

Principle 2: Build Down, Not Just Out
Recruitment is width; leadership is depth. Map your organisation by levels and identify where belief breaks. Reach down, run three-way leadership calls, and adopt the orphans whose sponsor went quiet.

Principle 3: Event-Anchored Growth
 Events are belief factories and non-negotiable. We run an Invite Blitz, set micro-commitments, then a 72-Hour Sprint so every attendee books three PS3s and a presentation.

Principle 4: Objection Systems
Keep a living document of top objections and the best tools or stories to match them. Practise until responses are natural.

Principle 5: Recognition With Teeth
Recognition without standards creates entitlement. Reward behaviours as well as outcomes.

Principle 6: Pace-Setting and Peace-Keeping
A leader wears two watches: speed and stability. Pace-setting means you're visibly producing. Peace-keeping means addressing conflict quickly and privately.

Myths That Keep People Small — and the Truths That Set Them Free

- Myth: "I don't have time."
  Truth: You have pockets. Ten minutes, done six times, beats one hour you never start.

- Myth: "I'm not confident enough."
  Truth: Confidence is the result of action, not the prerequisite.

- Myth: "I need a big audience."
  Truth: You need a clear message and consistent visibility. Ten conversations daily will beat ten thousand passive followers.

Case Study Snapshots From the Trenches

Snapshot 1: The Power of Firsts
A new partner joined on a Thursday. We set a 72-hour plan: first post that night, first invites Friday, first PS3 Saturday. By Monday she had two customers and three prospects booked. Early action crushed early doubt.

Snapshot 2: Depth Over Width
One leg stalled. I scheduled a weekly depth call for that leg only. Fifteen minutes, sharp. We focused on one skill per week. Within six weeks two new leaders emerged.

Content With a Spine: Showing Up Online Like a Leader

Social content is not the business, but it feeds the business. I use a simple rotation:

- Credibility (mini case studies, client wins, team stories)

- Connection (family moments, values, lessons learned)

- Conversion (clear calls to action)

- Community (shout-outs, gratitude, event recaps)

- Compass (what I believe and why)

I don't try to be viral; I try to be valuable. Value earns attention. Consistency earns trust. Trust earns conversations.

The Emotional Engine: Why You Must Choose Yourself

There will be mornings you won't want to send one more message and seasons when results lag. In those moments you need a Why that feels less like a slogan and more like a promise.

My promise was simple: My children will not inherit my limitations. That promise pulled me through the awkward firsts, the quiet months, the mistakes. It reminded me that patience is not passivity; it is persistence with perspective.

Choosing yourself is not arrogance. It is stewardship. You are responsible for the gifts you've been given.

Your Seven-Day Leader Sprint (Detailed Action Plan)

Day 1 — Audit & Architect

- Identify where you're waiting and choose one action.

- Build a Minimum Viable DMO.

- Block a power hour.

Day 2 — Pipeline & PS3

- Make a master list of 50 names.
- Send 10 Peek messages and book one Show.
- Line up a 3-way.

Day 3 — Follow-Up Framework

- Create three templates and follow up with every open thread.
- Log objections and pair each with a tool.

Day 4 — Content That Converts

- Post one authority piece and record value stories.
- Invite viewers to DM a keyword.

Day 5 — Depth & Adoption

- Offer two fifteen-minute coaching calls below your frontline.
- Teach one skill and help them book next actions.

Day 6 — Event Anchor

- Invite for a call, presentation, or meet-up within seven days.
- Confirm twice and send a calendar invite.

Day 7 — Review, Recognise, Reinforce

- Review numbers and identify the bottleneck.
- Recognise behaviour publicly and set next week's DMO.

Implementation Challenges (and How to Beat Them)

- Kids/caregiving: work in sprints; stack micro-wins.

- Unsupportive circle: demonstrate results, don't argue.

- Low energy: tie your DMO to triggers.

- Plateaus: double exposures before changing strategy.

What I Wish Someone Had Told Me

- The room you're in matters. Put yourself where the conversation is bigger than your excuses.

- Your story is an asset — even in progress. Share the struggle and the step you're taking.

- Hard seasons are part of the curriculum. Don't repeat the class by quitting early.

- Money follows mastery, and mastery follows monotony.

- You don't need to be chosen. You need to be consistent.

The Quiet Promise — Expanded & Strengthened

I didn't succeed because life rolled out a red carpet. I succeeded because I decided that my imperfect, messy, inconvenient circumstances were enough to start. I chose to learn in public, to act before I felt ready, and to make consistency my competitive edge.

I decided to lead without permission. First myself, then others.

And that's the invitation of this chapter. Not to wait for belief, applause, or the "right" time, but to choose yourself now, in this moment.

Send the first message. Book the first three-way. Show up to the event. Track the truth. Celebrate the micro-win. Do it while your hands are shaking, while your voice is unsure, while no one is watching.

Stack the next rep, and the next, and the next, until one day you look up and realise: the person you became along the way is worth more than the goal you were chasing.

Because the loudest results are always built in the quiet. The world doesn't need another person sitting on the sidelines, waiting to be picked. It needs you, moving daily, decisively, unapologetically, toward the life you were meant to lead.

And when they ask, "Where did you get the confidence?" you'll smile, because you'll know the truth:

I didn't wait for it to arrive.

I built it, one small, relentless, consistent day at a time.

"Whether you think you can or think you can't, you're right."

— Henry Ford

KAREN FETTES

Accolades

- Hit top of comp plan in 18 months

- Top 1% of company

- Consistent trip and incentive earner

- International downline on multiple continents

- Personally recruited 100 in 2023

THE POWER OF MINDSET IN PERSONAL RECRUITING: HOW I TRANSFORMED MY BUSINESS BY CHANGING MY FOCUS

Mindset Over Mechanics

Direct sales is a business of relationships, persistence, and personal growth. But it's not just a business. For me, it's been a personal growth journey disguised as a compensation plan.

After 16 years in this industry, I've learned that while strategy, skill, and effort matter, mindset is the single greatest factor in success.

I've experienced seasons of explosive growth as a top recruiter. I've had steady seasons of consistent, moderate recruiting. And I've faced seasons where I barely moved the needle. My business, like yours, has seen ups and downs. If I'm honest, my life has seen even more.

My son has endured eighteen brain surgeries. In 2021, my combat-injured husband survived a major heart attack. In just two years, we lost three parents and became full-time caregivers for our last surviving parent whose health was failing. Some days I felt so emotionally drained that running my business felt impossible, but I kept going.

I don't share this for sympathy. I share it because hard things happen to all of us. Life throws curveballs that could easily justify stepping back.

Sound familiar?

Every one of us has a story. Every one of us can list reasons why our business isn't where we want it to be. While those reasons are real, they don't have to define our results. Here's the truth: mindset is what separates those who accept defeat from those who rise.

Life is messy, unpredictable, and rarely easy. But when we push through the hard seasons, we build resilience that fuels extraordinary growth in the easier ones.

Coach's Notes – Rob & Frazer
Your ability to connect personal trials with business lessons makes this section so impactful. Leaders will see themselves in your story and feel encouraged to keep going no matter what life throws at them.

The Wake-Up Call

Despite everything I'd been through, I thought I was still holding it together in my business. I had a solid team, consistent sales, and years of experience. But recruiting? That was a different story.

In 2022, I sponsored one person the entire year. Yes, one. For someone who had built a thriving business, that wasn't just disappointing, it was unacceptable.

I knew something was off, but I kept brushing it aside. I told myself I was "busy with other things." I mentally blamed the market, social media algorithms, and timing.

I knew something had to change, but I didn't immediately dive into action. I analyzed. I reflected. And finally, I faced the uncomfortable truth:

I was the problem.

Owning the Problem

It's easy to blame external factors:

- No one is interested right now

- I'm too busy with family responsibilities

- People just aren't responding the way they used to

Sound familiar? I've said them all at one point or another.

But when I stripped away the excuses, I realized that my recruiting numbers weren't low because of market changes or lack of interest. I wasn't recruiting because I wasn't doing the work.

Recruiting wasn't a priority.
I wasn't initiating conversations.
I wasn't meeting new people.
I wasn't planting seeds or following up.

I had let life's challenges shift my focus away from one of the core activities that grows a business, and it showed.

The gap in my recruiting wasn't external. It was internal.

But here's the thing: you can change it. Right now. Today.

Coach's Notes – Rob & Frazer
This is a powerful mirror moment. Owning the problem instead of blaming circumstances is a leadership lesson in itself. Readers will feel challenged but also empowered by your honesty.

Why Mindset Matters More Than Strategy

Let me be clear: strategy is important. But mindset is the foundation.

You can have the perfect recruiting scripts, the best social media strategy, and all the tools at your fingertips. But if your mindset isn't aligned, none of that matters.

Here's why:

- Your mindset determines your energy, and energy is contagious.

- Your mindset shapes your confidence, and confidence attracts people.

- Your mindset drives consistency, and consistency is the secret to long-term success.

What we focus on expands.

Here's something I often remind my kids (and myself):

"You can't get upset about the results you didn't get from the work you didn't do."

The same holds true for direct sales.

When I looked at my low recruiting numbers, I couldn't be mad. I wasn't doing the work.

If you believe no one is interested, you won't share the opportunity.
If you believe recruiting is hard, you'll avoid it.
If you believe you're not good at sponsoring, you won't develop the skills.

The good news? You can change your mindset.

How I Shifted My Mindset (and Recruited 100 People in 10 Months)

In early 2023, I hit a breaking point and took a hard look at the facts in front of me. I decided to take responsibility and rebuild my mindset from the ground up. I dove headfirst into rewiring the stories I was telling myself. I personally sponsored 100 new team members in the 10 months that followed—after bringing in just one the previous year.

Here's exactly what I did, and what you can start doing today.

1. Speak to Yourself Like a Top Recruiter

Your inner dialogue is either your biggest cheerleader or your greatest saboteur.

I realized I had been reinforcing negative beliefs:

- "No one wants to join right now."

- "I don't know enough people."

- "I'm not good at sponsoring anymore."

I replaced those thoughts with intentional affirmations:

- "I am a magnet for driven, motivated recruits."

- "People want to partner with me because I am a great mentor."

- "I attract the right people at the right time."

When you believe in your ability to sponsor and lead, you exude the kind of confidence that draws others in.

Action Steps:

- Write down three affirmations that reflect the recruiter you want to become.

- Say them out loud every morning and before any business activity.

- Identify what drains you and shift focus to areas that reignite passion.

2. Focus on Serving, Not Selling

I shifted from "I need to grow my team" to "Who can I help today?"

I asked:

- "Whose life could this business change?"

- "Who needs community, purpose, or extra income?"

This subtle but powerful shift made conversations easier because I led with a heart of service, not desperation. I wasn't just "recruiting." I was helping solve problems.

Action Steps:

- Create a "Who Can I Help?" list.

- Ask more questions. Let prospects tell their story.

- Reach out and engage with them authentically.

- Focus on their needs first.

3. Reconnect with Your 'Why'

Let's be honest—if you're not excited about your business, no one else will be.

When I found myself in a slump, I had to fall back in love with the opportunity I was offering. I revisited the reasons I started. I made a list of everything this business had done for my family and me. That gratitude shifted my perspective. When you operate from a place of genuine belief and excitement, recruiting feels natural.

Action Steps:

- Write down three reasons why you love your business.

- Share those reasons in conversations, team meetings, and compliantly on social media.

- Create a vision board reflecting your goals and revisit it regularly.

- Reflect on the lives you've impacted and remind yourself of your influence.

4. Expand Your Comfort Zone and Your Network

Growth doesn't happen inside your comfort zone. I realized I needed to meet new people. Genuinely meet new people. This business is 100% about authentic relationships. I intentionally sought out new environments, joined groups, and started talking to people again. I focused on building relationships, not pitching. Not every relationship converts into a business prospect, and that's okay. We are humans and need human connection.

Over the past five years, I had become comfortable not leaving my house or engaging in real-world conversations. Once I started putting myself in new circles, doors began to open. Some of my best conversations came from unexpected places—a coffee shop, an airplane, a grocery store, even on vacation.

Action Steps:

- Join two new groups or communities in the next month.

- Engage on social media. Comment on posts, participate in group discussions, and share value-driven content.

- Commit to having one authentic, non-business conversation daily.

- Reach out to someone you already know—not about business, just to check in.

- Practice engaging with people outside your normal circles.

5. Embrace Rejection as Redirection

Not everyone will say yes, and that's okay. Rejection is part of the process, not a reflection of your worth. I used to take "no" personally. But I learned to reframe rejection as redirection. Every "no" brought me closer to someone who was the right fit. Some of the people who initially declined came back months later, ready to join. It wasn't about convincing them, it was about staying visible and consistent.

Here's a truth that might sting: the worst rejection isn't hearing "no," it's missing the opportunity to ask. It's not your job to decide if this business is right for someone. Your job is to share the opportunity and let them decide.

Action Steps:

- Track how many conversations you initiate each week—not just results.

- Set a goal for at least 10 conversations per week.

- Follow up without pressure. Timing is everything, and sometimes it just isn't right for them—yet.

- Create a "not now" list for those who aren't ready. Check in with them quarterly.

6. Refine Your Language and Confidence

I realized I needed to get comfortable talking about what I do and how I help others. Despite years of experience and success, I found myself stumbling over my words. I was proud of my business but struggled to articulate my value clearly. I started reintroducing myself not just as someone in direct sales, but as a top leader in an international direct sales company. I crafted clear "I help" statements that highlighted how I serve others.

For example:

- "I help military spouses build businesses they can take with them wherever life moves them."

- "I help parents of chronically ill children create businesses that allow them to work from home while being present for their kids."

- "I help realtors and service professionals curate custom client gifts that build lasting connections."

By redefining how I spoke about my business, I reignited my confidence and started attracting the right people.

Action Steps:

- Write your own "I help" statement that reflects your strengths and target audience.

- Practice introducing yourself confidently in both business and personal settings.

- Use your story authentically in presentations, posts, and conversations.

Coach's Notes – Rob & Frazer
This playbook is world-class. By breaking down exactly how you shifted your mindset and pairing each step with action items, you've given readers a blueprint they can immediately apply to transform their own results.

Final Thoughts: The Power of Daily Mindset Work

Recruiting is about empowering others, creating community, and changing lives—but you have to get your mindset right first. Your mindset, more than any script or strategy, will determine how far you go. It isn't a one-time shift, it's a daily practice.

Every morning, recommit to the belief that you are a powerful recruiter. Speak it, believe it, and most importantly, act on it.

The results will follow. You are capable of becoming a top recruiter. The only thing standing in your way is the story you're telling yourself.

Change the story, and you'll change your business.

"Leadership is not about being in charge. It's about taking care of those in your charge."

— Simon Sinek

LAURA LIPINSKI

Accolades

- Built a 6-figure network marketing business while raising 3 children

- Co-founder and leader of an international network in 30+ countries

- 20 years of experience mentoring leaders worldwide

THE HIDDEN LEADERSHIP GAP: AND HOW TO CLOSE IT BEFORE IT BREAKS YOUR TEAM

Introduction

A few months ago, I was lying flat on a ferry.
Not a holiday cruise. A brutal, 24-hour mal de mer, unable to move, drink, or eat.

And yet...
Sales kept coming in.
Clients got their products.
My team was moving forward without me touching a thing.

That is when I understood: this is what real leadership looks like.
Not being the hero who does everything.
But building leaders who keep the ship moving even when the captain is out.

Coach's Notes – Rob & Frazer
This opening is excellent. The image of your team moving forward while you were unavailable gives readers a crystal-clear picture of sustainable leadership. It's not about being the hero, it's about building systems and leaders who can carry momentum without you.

The Problem with Leadership in Network Marketing

In our industry, the word "leader" is overused.
Someone hits a rank, and suddenly, they are called a leader.

176

But titles do not make leaders.
A leader is someone who develops other leaders, not just someone who achieves results alone.

Too often, I have seen people at the top who are simply managing followers. When they step away, everything collapses. That is not leadership. That is dependency.

If you disappeared for two weeks, would your team keep growing? That is the simplest way to test the strength of your leadership.

Why I Do Not Believe in "Pochoir Leadership"

Many people come into this business searching for a template.
They want a step-by-step stencil: tell me exactly what to post, say, and do every day.

Yes, duplication is powerful for the basics. I give every new partner a simple 10-day plan for social media so they can start generating leads immediately.

But beyond that, leadership is not a one-size-fits-all stencil. Growth happens when you adapt the path to each individual.

I once worked with a distributor who kept asking me what to post every single day, months after she started. At some point, I had to tell her: "If you want me to think for you, you will never lead. My role is to help you find your own voice, not to hand you mine."

That is why my style is not to hold someone's hand forever, but to help them think, decide, and lead themselves.

Coach's Notes – Rob & Frazer
Your explanation of "Pochoir Leadership" is brilliant.

It challenges the over-simplified approach of giving everyone the same template. Leaders will take away that duplication has its place, but real leadership means creating independent thinkers, not permanent followers.

Action Steps:

When a new partner starts, give them a short duplication plan for the first 10–15 days, the things you know bring guaranteed results. For example, a simple daily posting plan for social media. But after that, adapt.

- Ask yourself: What are the actions I personally mastered that gave me predictable results?

- Write them down and turn them into a short starter plan (10–15 days) your team can copy-paste.

- After those first days, observe who starts getting results or shows leadership potential. With them, adapt the plan and help them grow beyond duplication.

☐ Why: Duplication is powerful at the start, because people need clarity and direction. But if you never move beyond it, you create followers instead of leaders. The goal is not to hold their hand forever, but to help them think, decide, and lead themselves.

The Leadership Gap

There is a dangerous gap in our industry.
People can rise quickly, sometimes by luck, without developing the maturity to sustain it.

It is like giving a 13-year-old the role of a parent. They might carry the title, but they do not yet have the capacity.

I know this gap well, because I fell right into it in my early years. I once pushed myself through a massive 90-day plan. On the surface, it looked incredible. The numbers were growing fast. Ranks were being hit. My ego was soaring. But behind the scenes, I was the only real leader. My team could follow my energy, but they did not yet have the maturity or the skills to sustain it. The moment I slowed down, everything fell apart.

And here is the trap. When we see this happening, the instinct is often to push people to recruit even more, believing that speed will fix everything. But it does not. Speed without maturity only amplifies the gap.

That experience taught me a painful but essential lesson. Speed can create growth. But without depth, it also creates fragility. Promoting people faster than they are prepared is not leadership. It is setting them up for failure.

That is why today, when I see rapid growth, I no longer celebrate only the volume. I look for maturity, responsibility, and readiness. Sometimes the smartest move is not to push for more, but to stabilize what is already there. Leadership gaps are not solved by acceleration. They are solved by education, mentorship, and time.

Coach's Notes – Rob & Frazer
This section nails a critical problem in our profession. Leaders reading this will see themselves in the trap of chasing speed. You offer them a better framework: depth, maturity, and responsibility before rapid growth. That shift alone can save teams from collapse.

Action Steps:

Every week, identify the fastest-growing people in your team, not just those recruiting fast, but also those generating steady sales or showing initiative. Then delegate small responsibilities to them.

Examples of responsibilities you can delegate:

- Co-hosting a team call

- Sharing their personal story in a meeting

- Answering questions in the group by pointing people to the right tools

- Collecting product testimonials in one place

- Taking charge of a small part of an event, such as welcoming guests or managing the product setup

☐ Why: If you, as the leader, keep all responsibility, you automatically create a leadership gap. Delegating early builds maturity step by step. It stabilizes the team and ensures growth is not just fast, but also sustainable.

Leadership as a Guide, Not a Manager

Our job is not to manage people. It is to guide them.

That means helping them see possibilities they do not yet see. Some leaders mistake delay for laziness. But often, the person is simply not ready. They cannot yet see the light you are shining.

I once watched a promising partner answer every single message her team sent. Late nights, early mornings, every problem landed on her shoulders. She thought she was being responsible. In reality, she was building dependency.

When someone messages me saying, "I did not get my package," my first question is, "What did customer service say?" Because my job is not to replace the company, the systems or the tools. My job is to teach people to think and act like leaders.

If you try to do everything for everyone, you will burn out. Worse: you will prevent your team from growing.

Action Steps:

Next time someone brings you a problem, ask them:

- "What have you already tried?"

- "What do you think we should do?"

- "What did customer service say?" (a slightly ironic reminder that they should have checked first).

The goal is to shift responsibility back onto them and build the habit of thinking and acting like a leader

☐ Here's why: Most of the time, when people ask for your answer, it's not because they don't know. It's because they lack confidence and are afraid their solution might be wrong. By asking their opinion first, you help them build the habit of making decisions, even small ones. That's how followers become leaders.

The 3 Pillars of My Leadership Approach

Deep Personal Development

Before you can lead others, you must lead yourself. That means knowing your values, building confidence without arrogance, and managing emotions under pressure.

I once coached a partner who froze at every conflict. She avoided hard conversations, hoping problems would solve themselves. Together, we worked on emotional resilience. Within six months, she was handling situations that used to paralyze her.

Action Steps:

Every week, take 10 minutes to face the areas you are avoiding.

Ask yourself:

- *What am I avoiding right now in my business?*

- *Why am I avoiding it? Is it fear, lack of confidence, or uncertainty?*

- *Who in my team or among my leaders could I talk to in order to move forward?*

☐ Decide one small action you can take this week to face it. It could be reaching out to that person, having the conversation you have postponed, or doing the task you keep delaying. Facing what you avoid is where your biggest growth as a leader is waiting

Continuous Mentorship Without Creating Dependency

I am present for my team, but not in a way that makes them rely on me for every decision.

When someone comes to me with a problem, my first question is: "What do you think we should do?" This shifts them from being order-takers to decision-makers.

Action Steps:

Before giving your answer, always ask your partner to propose at least two possible solutions and explain their reasoning.

- Encourage them to test their own idea and share the outcome afterward.

- Over time, this practice transforms them into decision-makers instead of order-takers.

Human-Centered Performance

Putting people first is not soft. It is smart. When people feel seen and valued, they deliver more.

I once worked with a partner making big income, holding a top rank, and constantly praised for performance. But in team groups, she rarely took initiative. She always waited for me or others to provide answers. That told me her maturity had not caught up with her results.

In contrast, I had another partner making a fraction of that income, but she consistently supported her team by looking for solutions and bringing ideas forward. Guess who I started preparing for bigger leadership roles?

Action Steps:

- At your next call, recognize someone not for volume but for initiative (for example: answering questions in the group, creating a resource, supporting a peer).

- At the same time, make sure recognition is balanced. Do not only reward people for management-style actions. This is still a business, and results matter.

- Write down three ways you can publicly reward both initiative and measurable progress this week.

- This keeps the culture people-centered, but still connected to business growth.

Avoiding the Duplication Trap

Duplication is essential at the start.
But believing that one system will work for everyone, at every stage, is a trap.

For beginners, I provide a clear 10-day plan so they can get early wins. For emerging leaders, I adapt based on their personality, strengths, and goals.

Some leaders think the solution to everything is a massive action plan. But not everyone is ready for that. Pushing someone into a sprint before they have the maturity is like asking a child to run a marathon. They may start fast, but they will collapse before the finish line.

And here is another reality: men and women often lead differently. Too often, male leaders try to coach women the way they coach men, and then wonder why women do not open up or advance. I have had many women in my team come to me privately, saying they did not feel understood by their male uplines. The same happens the other way around. If you ignore these dynamics, you will miss huge potential.

Action Steps:

- Review your last 3 coaching conversations with team members.

- Ask yourself: Were they actually effective? Did your guidance match their needs?

- Notice what they responded best to, and what they ignored or resisted.

- Look for patterns that show how your team reacts to different styles.

- Adjust your mentorship style to amplify what already works in the field instead of forcing what *you* believe should work.

Integrity Over Shortcuts

Leadership is not about quick wins at the expense of long-term trust.

I have seen methods that encourage people to take on debt, buy unnecessary packs, or chase hype with no substance. That is not leadership. That is manipulation.

Real leaders protect their people.
If your team knows you will never ask them to compromise their integrity, they will follow you for years, not just months.

Action Steps:

Before sharing a tactic, ask yourself: "Would I be proud if my child followed this?"

- If the answer is no, do not teach it.

- This week, review the last three tactics you promoted. Remove anything that risks trust for short-term numbers.

- Commit to building in a way you will be proud of in 10 years.

Action Items: Becoming a Leader Who Creates Leaders

- **Audit Your Leadership**
  If you disappeared for two weeks, would your team keep growing? If not, identify the bottlenecks.

- **Spot and Close the Leadership Gap**
  Identify potential leaders early and give them small responsibilities to prepare them for bigger roles.

- **Avoid the Pochoir Trap**
  Give clear structure for the basics, but personalize beyond that.
  There is no universal template once people move past the start.

- **Empower Through Questions**
  When someone comes with a problem, start with: "What do you think we should do?" Guide them to find their own answer.

- **Lead with Integrity**
  Never trade values for volume. Build in a way that you will be proud of in ten years.

Closing

Leadership is not about being the irreplaceable center.
It is about creating something that thrives without you.

It is about passing the torch so many times that one day, you realize:
you have lit up a whole city.

That is the kind of leadership that lasts.

*You can lead a horse
to water but you can't
make him drink.*

~ 12th century proverb

KAREN CLARK

Accolades

- Well known artist, educator, philanthropist, and intuitive lightworker

BEING OPEN TO POSSIBILITIES (ALIGNMENT)

Unlikely Alignment

I have been collecting water bottles for years, looking for one that had it all. I've tried special UV self-cleaning bottles, bottles that would open easily to hold ice, insulated, collapsible, mineral-adding—you name it, I tried it. I bought one or more of each of them to use every day. I wanted to replace the temporary bottles that add to the pollution of our environment. I even began researching filtering ones because I knew we were rapidly polluting every drop of water on the planet.

Then came a bottle that provided something new. Something that resonated with me—a combination of several metaphysical properties all working together with science-backed molecular hydrogen infusion and health rejuvenating features. I felt like I had hit the jackpot of water bottles! I was even compelled to sell this water bottle to everyone I cared about and then some.

I had been in network marketing before but was unsuccessful, and it seemed like even though I had a perfect product, I was heading in that same direction again. I could not even give the bottle away! I honestly could not understand why such a valuable item was not understood. Was I not aligned with this wonderful bottle after all, and should I walk away? Even though I had support, I did not feel like I was in charge. I wanted to do things the way I was shown, but with an added twist, a part of me that was genuine and heartfelt. I was working with many who did not resonate with this in the same way I did, and I almost gave up.

Coach's Notes – Rob & Frazer
Karen's honesty here is powerful. Most people never admit when they feel out of alignment, but that's where real breakthroughs come from. By sharing her struggle, she gives others permission to acknowledge their own.

Reading in research what I should do next, before considering walking away, required me to act as if I was the original person starting this. I held on and continued to pitch quietly, bringing the bottle everywhere, share it in the thirst-provoking Arizona summer.

While there, I connected with my therapy horse and learned about heart coherence, something that calms the body and soul and leaves one open for a better overall life. I noticed someone else pitching their product, and thought to myself no one needs more pitches at a retreat! So I concluded I would not share about this amazing water bottle unless someone asked. No one did.

Like leading a horse to the proverbial watering hole, I did not take the opportunity to share, to take that drink from possibility even for myself. I let someone else do so, and shrunk away.

So as a thank you, I sent a hydrogen water bottle to each of the hosts of the retreat. Since I believed in this one, I bought quite a few to share. All I said was, "I believe in this," and let it go. No work, no hype—just a gift.

Later, I received messages from the hosts independently saying they loved the water bottle and felt a difference, especially the owner of the horses. We struck up a conversation, and she wanted to sell the bottles because she resonated with what it had to offer, as did her fiancé!

I saw this as a chance to help with her dream—to build a permanent retreat house for the horses to connect with clients for longer periods of time. This was such an unlikely alignment, but here it was a couple of weeks after letting go: three people were interested in my dream, and I in theirs!

Coach's Notes – Rob & Frazer
This shows the magic of leading with belief instead of pressure. Karen didn't push. She gave from the heart, and that gift created alignment far stronger than a scripted pitch ever could.

Since I had a glimmer of hope now, I decided to attend the water bottle convention. I bought tickets for my spouse and my team, but no one could come with me. Even though I was sad at the prospect of going alone, I chose to show up and represent myself as a Tiny Team!

I thought I had qualified for the private CEO breakfast, but because my people didn't attend, I let fear take over and missed the opportunity. They had told me I could go, but I didn't. Once again, fear kept me from drinking at the proverbial well.

Not to dwell on what could have been, I created my own version. As CEO of my Tiny Team, I had a "private breakfast" in spirit form. With coffee, water bottle, muffin, pen, and paper, I held the meeting as if it were just as important as the one I missed. That's when the shift occurred—the shift that happens when you show up for yourself.

The therapy horse I had worked with came in spirit to this meeting, and in my vision even wanted to sell water bottles for humans and horses. Heart-to-heart coherence as the horse had taught me.

Later, I slipped a note to the owner of the company sharing my dream about the horse therapy retreat and our intertwined visions. She read it, and eventually told me we would be given access to the prototype for larger animals.

This unlikely alignment unfolded only because I chose to believe in myself, take small steps of faith, and let go of the rest.

It has been a while since then. We had a meet and greet with the horse owner, my sponsor, and me via video call, and introduced the horses. She loved the idea of one horse having his own account to raise money for his retreat center. She even announced that he would be signed up to sell bottles for his cause. Tiny Team signed him up, and the rest is history.

Coach's Notes – Rob & Frazer
Karen's story reminds us that alignment isn't about forcing results. It's about stepping into courage, taking the sip when it presents itself, and letting your belief open the doors you can't predict.

Action Items

- **Share from the heart, then let go.** Timing creates alignment far more powerfully than hype.

- **Be ready for opportunity.** It often shows up when you least expect it.

- **Rejection is redirection.** A closed door is usually an invitation to something better.

- **Stay open to what seems unlikely.** What looks impossible can unfold when you believe.

- **Trust that your vision exists beyond what you can see.** Step into it now and let it manifest.

"Our deepest fear is not that we are inadequate. Our deepest fear is that we are powerful beyond all measure."

– Marianne Williamson

DR. KAREN C. DWIRE, OTD

Accolades

- 16 years of network marketing experience

- Featured guest speaker at Accessibility Events and OT conferences

- Founded Accessible Travel Planners in 2023

- One of the fastest to reach first leader position in travel network marketing (10 months)

THE PROFIT WITH PURPOSE BLUEPRINT: HOW TO GROW A BUSINESS THAT GIVES BACK

The Night Everything Changed

In the wee hours of December 29, 1995, I died.

I had just turned 18. Everything was lined up—college, beauty, love, friends, and acceptance into my first-choice school. But in an instant, my life, body, and face shattered beyond recognition. What came next was almost beyond description: a brief yet timeless freedom from human form, followed by a return into pain and brokenness.

It was Winter Break of my senior year in my hometown of Grand Junction, Colorado. I was driving around to different holiday parties with a friend. I had been accepted to Colorado State University's pre-Occupational Therapy program. I was tall, athletic, attractive, smart, in love, and excited for the future.

And then it all shattered.

My 1983 Chevy Cavalier veered off the road and slammed into an embankment. No airbags or cell phone in 1995. My face slammed against the steering wheel. My legs were crushed as the floor crumpled beneath me—my foot still on the gas. I remember nothing of the crash. My last memory was five minutes before, pulling away from a party.

As this happened, I left my human form and became a whispering vapor. I became breath—the kind you can see on a cold night. I floated in the stillness of the winter air, weightless and shapeless. My body lay below, broken and lifeless, while I danced and dipped in the ether. Time no longer existed. It wasn't scary. It was peaceful and deeply beautiful.

Then earthly reality began to creep in, like the moment between sleep and awake. I don't know if I chose to return or if something deeper chose for me, but I came back to pain, loss, and the greatest challenges of my young life.

I returned slowly, sense by sense—blind, broken, bleeding, and hypothermic. My passenger, Jason, a childhood friend, was unconscious with a severe brain injury. I knew he'd die if no one found us, so I crawled on my back, elbows digging into the frozen ground, half-blind and in agony, inching up the embankment. Over two hours later, I flagged down a Pepsi truck. One of the men inside had the last name Miracle, which is exactly what they were.

I begged them to find Jason. They did—and found him alive. That moment was the greatest relief of my life. Jason made a full recovery. He's now a civil engineer with three kids.

Coach's Notes – Rob & Frazer
This opening is unforgettable. The vivid detail of your near-death story grabs the reader and instantly sets the stage for the purpose-driven message you carry throughout the rest of the chapter.

Turning Pain Into Purpose

My recovery was long. Dozens of reconstructive surgeries, months of rehabilitation, and an identity reshaped by scars. But I walked at graduation, started college on time, and became an Occupational Therapist.

As an OT, I quickly realized that traditional healthcare wasn't for me. Bureaucracy, politics, and red tape weighed me down. I became a traveling therapist, which gave me some freedom, but still no purpose and no path to long-term financial or time freedom.

That came later.

In 2009, my husband at the time was diagnosed with coronary artery disease and required six stents. A friend introduced us to products she believed could help. We hesitated, but tried them. The results convinced us. What we didn't expect was that network marketing would also be the answer for our financial health and, ultimately, our time freedom.

We went to an event, and just like that, I discovered network marketing and the power of community, duplication, and residual income.

At that event, I met Kathrine Lee, a top earner who had also co-founded the Pure Hope Foundation with her husband Michael, a sanctuary for survivors of human trafficking. Her network marketing income funded her life so that all donations to the nonprofit went directly to its mission. That was the most beautiful blend of purpose and profit I'd ever seen.

I visited the Pure Hope Ranch twice. It was the most peaceful place I've ever experienced. On my second visit, my vision became clear: I wanted to create massive change too.

Coach's Notes – Rob & Frazer
Your story about Kathrine Lee is a powerful example of what's possible when profit fuels purpose. It shows leaders the bigger picture of why this profession matters beyond income.

The Birth of Accessible Travel Planners

Later, after a divorce and distance from the company, I discovered the travel industry. Even better, I found a network marketing company in travel. My heart lit up. I enrolled the same day.

Most of the people who joined me were OTs and PTs. We asked: what if we could help people with disabilities, chronic illness, and special needs travel better?

That was the seed of Accessible Travel Planners (ATP). It began as a Google Doc and a Zoom call. From a single course, it grew into a thriving community. In two years, hundreds of travel agents have trained with us, and our reach is now over 1,000 professionals worldwide.

Now, I'm transitioning ATP into a nonprofit to fund travel for those who otherwise couldn't experience it. Our mission: help people of all ages and abilities travel freely, safely, and without limits. Because I am self-funded by my network marketing business, all the money ATP generates is reinvested into the mission.

Coach's Notes – Rob & Frazer
This section beautifully connects your personal passion with a real-world solution. Leaders will take away how aligning with purpose creates effortless attraction and momentum.

The Profit with Purpose Blueprint: 3 Keys

1. Lead with Mission vs. Marketing

When you lead with purpose, you shift the entire energy of your business. People don't just want what you offer, they want to be part of what you stand for.

In a noisy world of funnels and formulas, it's your why that cuts through. Customers become collaborators. Team members become advocates. Purpose is the new marketing.

2. Build a Community, Not a Downline

In occupational therapy, we talk about doing, being, becoming, and belonging. When you build a community, you give people belonging.

This isn't about recruitment—it's about relationships. When people feel seen, supported, and stretched, momentum happens naturally.

3. Let Impact Drive Income

When your work changes lives, income becomes evidence of transformation. Purpose carries you through slow starts and quiet seasons. Profit is not the goal—it's the byproduct of consistent, mission-driven work.

Why Isn't Everyone Doing This?

Many people are conditioned to believe that helping others means sacrificing their own wealth. They think they must choose: serve or succeed.

But it's not either-or. Service can be the very source of sustainable income. And income can become the fuel to serve even more.

A Call to Action

Look at your business. Could it be more than a paycheck? Could you use your products or platform to support a cause? Don't wait until you have more time or money. Start now. Do it messy, do it scared, but do it. Let your heart lead the way.

A Warning

Not everyone will understand your mission. Some will criticize. Others will walk away. I even got terminated by one travel network marketing company because of ATP. Don't let it harden you. Keep your heart soft and your purpose strong. Let go of those who drift away. New friends, new impact, and new purpose await on the other side of that decision.

My Final Question to You

If you died today—just like I did 30 years ago—and had to choose whether to come back, what kind of life would make that choice worth it?

CONCLUSION

If you've made it to this point, you've just absorbed wisdom from some of the sharpest leaders in the profession. And my hope is this: you don't just read it but also that you use it.

Every single person who contributed to this book is proof that leadership isn't about titles, timing, or talent. It's about consistency, ownership, and the courage to grow when it would be easier to coast.

You'll notice the common threads. They did the work when it wasn't convenient. They faced setbacks and still kept going. They built people, not just paychecks. And that's why they're here — still leading, still growing, still building legacies.

So here's my challenge to you: Don't let this book become another thing that sits on your shelf. Choose one idea and act on it before the week is over. Then choose another. And another.

Because leadership isn't built in one big leap. It's built in the daily habits, the conversations you keep having, and the example you keep setting.

I'll finish with this: Our profession doesn't just need more *leaders*. It needs more builders. People willing to go first, to show the way, to duplicate what works, and to keep the flame of momentum alive.

That's what this book is about. That's what your business is about. And that's the kind of leader you can choose to be starting now.

— Rob Sperry

www.ingramcontent.com/pod-product-compliance
Lightning Source LLC
Chambersburg PA
CBHW071603210326
41597CB00019B/3377